An honest and fascinating journey of a spiritual pioneer recounting the many joys and heartrending challenges of her calling. Beautifully written, tugs at your heartstrings!
Marie Ang, B.S., Elementary Education
Former child-care coordinator, Unification Theological Seminary

This is the story of a courageous woman who found her "soul call" was to extend her mother's heart beyond her immediate family to promote healing and growth among individuals, couples and communities around the world. The cost was not small, but the impact was deep.
Sharon Goodman, B.A. Early Childhood Education and Art,
Former Principal, Pu'ukumu School, Kauai, Hawaii

Reading my mother's memoir, I am reminded that my siblings and I are the children of a truly remarkable woman whose love for God and others is uncommonly deep. She writes that one particular time when she would be separated from us to serve in a mission, she promised God that when her children grew up we would see two parents who loved God and loved each other and who would be there for us for the rest of their lives.
Well, mom, you have kept your promise.
Matthew Jones, Eldest son
Attorney, Kim and Chang, Seoul, Korea

With humor and compassion, Betsy shares her unique journey to discover what God wants. As she attempts to heal hearts near and far, her own heart grows. Could this be what God wants for all of us?
Therese Stewart, Ed.D
Academic Dean – Ret., Unification Theological Seminary

This is the story of a divine call heard by a young child and her lifelong effort, in every circumstance, to respond. You will be inspired to inquire within to find your own source of direction, purpose, and love- to listen deeply for your own clear call.

Anne Edwards, MSW
Social Services Administrator, Editor

This is a compelling love story between two people, Betsy and Farley, who had in common a love of God and who were the beneficiaries of God's synchronic grace. It seems to me that Father Moon wanted to bring more love into the world, and so did Betsy and her husband. I admire their goals; this book recounts Betsy's remarkable journey in a heart-touching way.

John B. Jenney, Esq.
Former Magistrate, Norfolk (MA) County Probate
and Family Court, Former Maryknoll Seminarian

Betsy tells her story of mission, marriage, parenting and spiritual awakenings in a straight-forward style, trusting in the narrative itself to convey its power. She succeeds, moving the reader's heart with every turn of the page. Within the covers of this beautiful book lies a quiet and confident wisdom born from experience, certainly a rare commodity in our noisy world.

Jeffrey Scharfen, Esq.

Answering the Call

My Spiritual Journey

Betsy Jones

For information:
Peaceful Center Publishing
email: betsyj777@aol.com

Production and creative:
jonathangullery.design@gmail.com

FIRST EDITION

ISBN Print: 979-8-9858550-0-5
ISBN Ebook: 979-8-9858550-1-2

Printed in the United States of America

Contents

*Take your mistakes as lightly as you may,
set them as naught. Rejoice more in My Love
than sorrow in your often failing.*
—Julian of Norwich

Be still and know that I am God.
—Psalm 46:10

*God invites us to become His most intimate
companion and sharers of the divine nature,
and He does everything possible to get us there.*
—Thomas Keating

*Your heart is your closest teacher. In the face
of difficulty or confusion, ask your heart.
Your Heavenly Parent who loves you resides
deep in your heart. You are designed
to hear God's true voice.*
—Hak Ja Han Moon

*To my husband Farley, my children
Matthew, Cara, Harvet, Bow and Farley,
to my daughters-law Yunhee and Kori,
my son-in-law Don, our grandchildren
and all those on earth and in heaven
who have guided me on my path:
each one of you is precious to me.
I thank each of you for your
presence in my life.*

In loving memory of those who were called young:

Heung Jin Moon (10/23/1966-1/2/1984)
David Linn Ang (12/6/1970 – 1/4/1992)
Andrew Walrick Byrne (10/20/1984-6/3/2001)
Homer Charles Boutte (5/2/1982-11/2003)

Acknowledgements

I offer heartfelt thanks to my husband Farley for his patient investment in helping me express this story: to my son Matthew, to my daughter Cara, and to friends Thomas Ward, Marie Ang, Nora Spurgin, Therese Stewart, Biff Jenney, Jeff Scharfen and Sharon Goodman, all of whom gave thoughtful comments benefitting this work. Also, Anne Edwards' wordsmith skills and structural recommendations were invaluable, and Jonathan Gullery offered outstanding layout and design services. Mike Welch, and the members of my memoir class which he led, gave me very useful support and feedback along the way. I thank all of these special persons for their kind and generous assistance.

Prologue

Guided by my mother as a young child I said prayers at night and attended Mass on Sundays. At Mass I loved the sacred music sung by the choir; hearing it, my spirit would soar.

The nuns at St. Joseph's grammar school in Waltham, MA taught of a loving God who was waiting to have a relationship with His children. My third-grade teacher told the story of a boy who regularly visited church, mentioning his name each time: "Jesus this is Jimmy." I caught the idea and would be drawn to stop at the church near St. Joseph's. "Dear God, this is Betsy." Sitting there in silence for some time, I would often sense a Presence with me. I would also feel some internal relief, as if this Presence had been waiting for me and appreciated my visit.

Over time, my sense of a personal relationship with God would grow.

I also found an outdoor location, on a curb around the corner from our house, that I designated as "my spot." In warm weather I would sit there, oblivious to cars passing by and other sounds around me. I was settled into a quiet interior space.

Twelve years of instruction by nuns had a continuing impact. I came to know they prayed several times a day, that some of them modeled themselves on the lives of saints, and that they had all chosen to offer their lives to God. I saw that they did not have financial wealth but that they had a type of spiritual wealth and happiness. In time I saw them as having freedom to be with God. That way of being struck an internal chord.

In my senior year in high school, a new feeling slowly emerged – the feeling that there was something I was supposed to do for God.

Then and thereafter, I would pray for direction. What is it, God? What do you want?

Through the twists and turns of college and graduate school the question would continue to haunt me.

Ultimately, an answer would come.

This is the story, as I see it, of my search for what God wanted.

1

The Calling

Marilyn

On a spring day in 1957 my older sister Marilyn handed me an envelope. "Betsy," she said, please read this letter." At the time we were sitting opposite each other on our beds in our room on the second floor of our cozy home in Waltham, Massachusetts.

I was then in the eighth grade and Marilyn in the twelfth, soon to graduate.

In the years prior to this moment, I had observed her on many an afternoon place a small white cloth, a mantilla, on her head and retreat into my parent's bedroom for, as she called it, "mental prayer." Once our parents' bedroom door was closed, I knew not to bother her.

I quietly opened the letter and read its shocking contents. "You're going into the convent?" I asked. "You're going to be a nun?"

My big sister, my only sister, was leaving home.

"You won't be going to college? You won't be visiting us?"

The thing was, wearing a mantilla was not my sister's only identity. She had been the queen of her senior prom. She had been the co-captain of the cheerleaders. She had captured the interest of more than one young man.

Now…a nun?

Still, knowing her at-home behavior, I could understand her choice. In time I would try to feel happy for her.

On another level, I grieved. She had been so much part of my life. Sleeping in the same room, swimming to a Cape Cod dock, skiing down a New Hampshire mountain. She was my companion and, as my older sister, my security. In our separate beds, I always felt better when she slept facing me.

My parents approved her decision but did not like the timing. Marilyn was only eighteen. She should be older before making such a commitment. She should go to college.

Trying to tease her away from her plan, they offered her a car.

To no avail.

In due course a black trunk appeared in our bedroom, progressively filled by our mother with the list of things – black stockings, black shoes, necessary underwear – Marilyn was to bring to the convent. The trunk was a type of dowry; it was accompanied by a monetary sum, as I recall $400.

In early summer the dreaded day finally came. Expecting that I would travel with Marilyn and my parents to the convent, my mother asked me several times to get ready. I didn't. To me my sister's departure felt like a death. I knew if I were to get in the car, I would just wail all the way to the convent.

Hugging my sister as she headed out our front door, tears welled up. And when the car pulled out of our driveway my tears became a torrent. I sat alone on our home's front steps and allowed myself to feel my sadness.

For a year or two thereafter, each time some family friend asked, "How is your sister?" my eyes would fill with tears.

My parents and I could visit her once a month in a public

meeting room shared with other families. At the two-hour mark a bell would ring, Marilyn would bid us farewell and would be among the first to exit the room. For me, each visit felt way too short.

Mom

My mother gave birth to four children, of which I was the third. Two of my siblings, including a brother before me and a sister after me, never lived past the first week.

For her third baby my mother was advised to undergo a caesarean section and told that she could choose the date. She chose June 3rd, the birth date of her dear sister Elizabeth, called Betty, who had died young. I was born on Betty's birth date and named after her. For the first years of my life, I was also called Betty.

Growing up, I would sometimes feel that I was not only my mother's daughter; I was also her sister.

Despite the sadness of losing two children, my mother would carry on her life with a distinct *joie de vivre*. This included a seemingly inexhaustible capacity to spend time with me. Sitting kitty corner at the small maple wood table in the middle of our kitchen, she would sip coffee, serve me tea with sugar and cream (she called it "little girl's tea"), and converse with me at length. Often, in addition to the beverages, we would share an orange. On many occasions by the end of our conversation she had eaten not only the orange, but also the peel. My comment, "Mom! You've eaten the whole thing!" seemed to surprise her. "Oops! Looks like I did." I think my comment was not an observation she was expecting from her five-year-old daughter.

Our connection was forged in other spaces as well. There was the piano in our basement and the organ in the living room. With her sitting at the piano and me right next to it, she would enthusiastically launch into the Fats Domino classic "Darktown Strutters' Ball." She would play, we both would sing, and with rhythmic feet, swaying hands and a happy heart, I would dance.

One time through the song was never enough.

There was not only fun. Mom was a devout Catholic, the president of the women's group -known as "Sodality" - in our local church. She made earnest efforts to pass her faith on to Marilyn and me. This meant regular attendance at Sunday mass ("Hurry everyone; we don't want to be late."), sending us to Catholic schools ("You get more discipline there.") and informal instruction for my sister and me as she stood pointing to a picture of Jesus which hung on her bedroom wall ("This is the sacred heart of Jesus. He suffered so much for us.")

The teaching from my mother was awkward, sometimes producing giggles from her two daughters. "Please listen," she exclaimed. "This is important!"

Dad

From my mother I inherited faith. From my father I inherited a love of outdoor activities. Dad brought me into the creation and introduced me to creative ways of interacting with it.

He was born in Halifax, Nova Scotia, where his father Duncan managed a skating arena and fathered eight children during his too short life. Duncan died from injuries suffered in what is known as the Great Halifax Explosion – the explosion of a munitions ship in the town harbor in 1917. My father was then about nine years old.

After my grandfather's death, my grandmother, Martha O'Neill, moved to Arlington, MA, bringing my father and his seven siblings with her.

My father was a lover of nature and of experiences in it. He introduced me at age five to skiing, starting on small local slopes, which he called" bunny hills," in and around our hometown of Waltham, a suburb of Boston.

Having grown our ski legs locally, my father one day announced to Marilyn and me that we now were to graduate from a hill to a mountain.

"Follow me across this way and don't look down the mountain." Those were Dad's instructions after we had been lifted the top of a ski slope on New Hampshire's Cranmore Mountain.

Unfortunately, his guidance on not looking down came too late. I had already seen what looked to me like a very steep slope. This was a novice trail? Still, mustering up my courage, I put my poles in the snow and launched into a type of traverse across the mountain, following my sister to where Dad had skied. "Now put your skis in a snow plow position, slowly turn and shift the weight to your downhill ski. I'll show you." I watched.

Not at all sure that I would keep control, my knees and ankles trembling, I took off. Well, the technique worked, and I made it to where Dad was. Whew!

I learned with further efforts that if I started losing control, I could swerve into the mountain to stop and even fall. After twenty or so of these horizontal traverses, and now much closer to the bottom, further guidance: "From here you can go straight down." Following Dad and Marilyn, and ready to chance it, I let go. Feeling the wind in my face and seeing the sun on the snow, I whooshed to the bottom. What a thrill. "I did it!"

And in the years since, including to the present, I have done it many times.

In the summer we went to Cape Cod for two or three weeks. Having a friend there who owned a boat and who was willing to lend it to any colleague who would pay for the gas, my father introduced us to water skiing. With him at the helm, I learned to ski on one ski, jumping the wake, waving happily at my smiling father. He in turn would give us a thumbs-up, obviously pleased over what he was able to offer his daughters.

My father shared his love not just with our family. At the Cape he regularly invited large groups to our small house for pots of steamed clams.

Not long after Marilyn left for the convent, on an occasion when my parents and I were sitting around our small kitchen table, the 1950's song "Daddy's Little Girl" began playing on the radio. "You're the end of the rainbow," the lyrics went, "my pot of gold, you're daddy's little girl to have and to hold…" Listening to the song, we all burst into tears, but especially my father. How much he missed his first-born daughter! Later he would tell my mother and me that beginning with the time my sister entered he would toot his horn seven times as he passed the convent on his way home from work. He hoped she would hear him, but he never knew.

In any case, he continued honking.

While my mother's style was more direct, my father offered me a type of freedom to choose my own way. At one point when I was studying a lot, not coming out of my room except for meals, he visited my room. "Betsy, this is not a library," he opined. "You should be out enjoying your life." Despite the input, the tone and humor in his voice told me any decision was mine.

His flexibility would later help me when I was making decisions inconsistent with the hopes and dreams my mother held for her second daughter.

Learning to water ski, snow ski, and love the outdoors gave me a connection to a spiritual dimension I would not have known without my father, and it gave me confidence – an inner voice that still says, "yes, you can do this!" These gifts have sustained me.

Saint Mary's

As I moved through school, my parents were always there, proud of my achievements, and proud of who their second daughter was becoming. My mother, especially, was happy that I seemed to be following a clear Catholic path.

Like my sister I integrated myself into the spiritual and social life of Waltham's Saint Mary's high school. I was blessed to have many friends, excel academically, qualify for the National Honor Society, and hold several leadership roles.

One friend, in particular, became important. Margie was from a devout Catholic family of six children; I joined their large family for meals, and Margie joined our small one for trips to the mountains in winter and to the Cape in summer. I adopted their family as a second one, came to admire their loving dynamics, and gained a vision of something I would want in my future.

Through four years of high school, however, my sister's choice was never far from my mind. Despite my own vision, was I in fact to follow her?

My time at St. Mary's would see a blossoming of the spiritual seed planted earlier, nurtured by the continued support of my mother and by the guidance of the Sisters of Notre Dame de Namur. There was daily religious instruction, introductions to the lives of the saints and encouragement to undertake extra-curricular reading. Thomas Merton's "The Seven Story Mountain" was high on the list. Like an empty sponge, I absorbed it all.

In my senior year I became the president of the St. Mary's

branch of Sodality.

In that role, the Sisters sometimes nudged me. At a school dance that Spring, a nun pulled me aside as my date and I glided cheek to cheek around the floor: "Leave enough space between you for the Holy Spirit," she advised. "Be an example to others." Slightly embarrassed, I took the guidance but laughed with my date as I reported it to him. Thereafter, we dutifully made more space.

There was a particular reason for my being an exemplar that night. In the front of the auditorium stood a large statue of Jesus' mother Mary, a statue that each May would be crowned with a colorful wreath of roses. That year, as Sodality's president, it was I who was to so honor her. Halfway through the dance, with the lights turned up and everyone circled around the statue, I made my way up a shaky ladder and placed the wreath on her head.

I was pleased to perform the deed, but relieved to get off that ladder.

I was one of perhaps twenty-five students in my class at a time when students stayed in the same room with the same teacher all day long. We would sit with our desks in straight columns, facing the teacher sitting behind a broad, wooden desk in the front of the room.

In the spring of my senior year my teacher, Sister Gertrude Francis, signaled me to come up front to speak with her.

Sister Gertrude was a warm, caring nun whose intelligence, teaching ability and apparent spiritual sensitivity I admired. Approaching her desk, I wondered the reason for her summons. "Betsy," she began, "have you ever thought you might have a vocation?"

A vocation?

I understood she meant a calling to be a nun.

"Please think about it." she continued. "If you have such a calling, and if you turn your back on it, you may never be happy."

I took in her message, thanked her and returned to my seat. Sitting there, my head began to spin. "Does she really think I should also enter a convent? What if I don't?"

From that time on the question of what God wanted me to do with my life began to haunt me. I asked for guidance: "God, what should I do? Please, give me signs."

2

Boston College
and Beyond

Prior to my conversation with Sister Gertrude, I was planning to be a nurse. I had applied to two three-year nursing schools and, on the wise advice of my mother, one four-year school. I was accepted at one of the three-year schools and, to my great surprise, also at the four-year program at Boston College. Surprised, because my scores on the college board exams were less than impressive.

I was strongly inclined to take advantage of my acceptance at Boston College, but a question nagged: "Is college what God wants of me? Or is it the convent?"

I resolved the issue by deciding to give B.C. a try for one year and then figure out the next step.

It turned out to be a great year. In its early months, several new friends suggested I run for president of the freshman nursing class. Overcoming my initial reluctance, I took the challenge. With the help of paper bookmarks produced by my father and inscribed with the slogan "Vote for Bets, She's the Best," I campaigned and won. Also, during the year I realized that taking care of patients - mind, body and soul - could be a type of spiritual work. That spoke to my longing.

By year's end I felt I had been given an answer to the question of God's will: the happiness that had come to me told me that B.C. was my right place, at least for now. I would continue there and watch for further signs.

Meeting Farley

Toward the end of my first year in college I had paid a visit to the administration office looking for ideas on summer employment. There I bumped into the registrar, a friendly woman named Kathy, standing behind a reception counter. In response to my employment question, she looked pensively at me for a moment and then suddenly brightened up. "Ah! Spring Lake!"

Spring Lake? What's that?

Kathy went on to explain that Spring Lake was a small town on the New Jersey shore, the location of a massive resort hotel known as the Essex and Sussex. The hotel typically hired college students as waitstaff for the summer and included housing.

A summer at the New Jersey shore? A place to stay? And make money?

Excited, I set about recruiting classmates to sign up, including my friend from New Jersey, Ginny. Ginny, it turned out, knew the hotel, known locally as the "E & S." She and I and perhaps four other classmates signed up. My friend Carol from high school, now at Boston College's School of Education, joined in.

That summer I eagerly tried my hand at waiting tables, cautiously tried body-surfing, and tentatively tried drinking, doing none of them very well.

Sometime in July a fellow waiter managed to arrange a double-blind date for Carol and me with two young lifeguards from a different hotel. Seeing them approach the waitstaff dormitory, Carol and I discussed who would be with whom. Having met our dates, we headed across the street to an ice cream parlor, where Carol sat with Farley and I with Sheldon.

While that evening was the last for Sheldon and me, for Carol and Farley it was a start; they dated for the next three years.

Five years later, I would meet Farley again.

Jamaica

In the spring of my junior year several recent graduates of the nursing school returned from a "Lay Missionary" experience in New Mexico and spoke to the nursing student body. In the combined roles of nurse and lay missionary they had provided both physical care and spiritual ministry to people in need.

The work they described resonated deeply with me. It offered me a way to respond to my ongoing question of God's will. When I graduated, I would not enter a convent; rather I would become a lay missionary. That is what I would do for God.

Senior year, I applied to Boston College's Lay Missionary program. The following spring, I was accepted, and left upon graduation with my friend Ginny for a year of service in Jamaica, West Indies.

My time in Jamaica was precious. Even now, over fifty years later, I easily access many images and feelings: the Jamaican people with their British accents, speaking and living with dignity; the children's sparkling eyes and bright smiles contrasting dramatically with their black skin; the Jamaican children calling me Miss Pepsi; families of six or more squished together in one room shacks, yet never complaining about their poverty; the islanders keeping the space inside and outside their homes well swept; the red, juicy mangoes growing plentifully throughout the island, and breadfruit and ackee as well; the people raising faithful voices on Sunday mornings, singing praise to God with a joyous spirit.

Ginny and I were assigned to a parish run by Franciscan priests who asked us to be available for home visits in an area called Maverley. Also, we were to provide nursing care at four schools - two each - in another area of Kingston.

Maverley was characterized by dirt roads and one room dwellings with small yards embracing tropical trees and outdoor stone cooking rings. Despite obvious poverty a happy spirit prevailed, nurtured no doubt by the beautiful blue skies, warm sun and year-round welcoming climate.

I lived with my fellow missionaries in a former church rectory. Having been provided a car but having limited access to it, I would walk each morning a mile and a half along dusty roads to my first school. When I arrived, the initial order of business involved helping a Jesuit priest mix powdered milk and water in a large vat, enough ultimately to pour a glass for each of the school's 300 students. Many of them had no breakfast.

Many students would arrive with both empty stomachs and wounded feet. Shoes and socks were rare commodities. Taking advantage of my training and providing needed nursing care to young children: this was deeply gratifying.

Some students liked to escape from their classes, coming to the nurse's office with made-up complaints. There they vied with each other to tell me stories and braid my hair. I felt their gentle touch not only on my head, but also in my heart.

Ginny and I were not in Jamaica in any official medical capacity; nevertheless, we drew on our backgrounds. Since medical supplies were in short supply, we sought contributions. One big-hearted owner of a large pharmacy opened his doors wide, giving us a shopping cart and permission to raid his shelves. With our fast hands filling the cart, it felt like Christmas.

Our care extended not only to children but to anyone who needed us. One day we answered an urgent knock on our door to learn that a local midwife had disappeared while her patient was giving birth. Scrambling to don our public health uniforms, dash to our car and start to back out the driveway, we suddenly realized we had different opinions about the distance from a baby's abdomen its umbilical cord was to be cut. One of us ran back in the house to grab our obstetrics textbook.

At least we would do no harm.

Arriving at a small cabin, we saw the mother sitting upright in her bed. Fully delivered, the baby was now lying between his mother's knees with the umbilical cord still attached. We boiled our surgical scissors, cut the cord at an agreed-on spot and somehow tied it.

Grateful for our service and aware of her limited resources, the mother asked us if we would like to keep the baby. There was no question of that, but as an alternative we told her we would be happy to provide a name.

Somewhere in Jamaica is a man called Michael Thomas, named after the two young men Ginny and I were fond of at the time.

———

Since my mission was to care not only for the body but also for the soul, one of the local priests arranged for me to have a room in each of my schools to teach classes on Catholic doctrine to adults.

I taught but also learned. A grandmother, who was taking care of her daughter's five children all day, once commented to me that she would be unable to do so "except for God's love."

The comment touched me. I was to strengthen the Jamaicans' faith, but experiences like this strengthened mine.

Despite such meaningful moments, in time I came to sense something missing. I thought my mission in Jamaica would satisfy my spiritual longing, to the point that I first considered extending my stay to five years. But after six months I began to feel my calling was beyond Jamaica. Service as a lay missionary was not my final answer.

At the same time, I started to feel disconnected from my fellow missionaries; this was a new experience for one who considered connecting with people as one of her strengths. Now I was distancing myself from people who had been my friends in both high school and college. Why?

I didn't know.

I turned to books.

I had become friends with Ronald, a Chinese man who, when his bushy hair was included, came up to my shoulder. Ronald was a gentle soul who owned a small bookstore in Kingston and loved to talk about books. During my final months in Jamaica, he opened his bookstore to me, allowing me to borrow as many books as I wanted.

And that was quite a few. I estimate I may have read as many as forty books during those months and borrowed even more.

I continued my work in the schools and in the parish, but my real interest was in deepening my understanding of spiritual realities. So, while continuing my mission work, I began reading a range of theologians and spiritual teachers, some rather advanced for me. My efforts included such authors as Paul Tillich and Hans Kung, as well as further reading of Thomas Merton.

I set myself a daunting task. Could I understand the truths

contained in these books?

On a sheet of paper, I made a list of the books I borrowed and inscribed two adjacent columns. The first column got a check when I finished a book and the second got a check if I felt I understood it.

A number of books challenged me. Those I would re-read. Most of them got a second check.

Having become in Jamaica an even more serious searcher, I found in Ronald's bookstore a welcome oasis.

About a year later an experience in a different bookstore would open a new door on my spiritual journey.

I had thought that being a lay missionary within the Catholic faith would lead me to feel I had accomplished whatever it was I was to do for God.

But it didn't, and I began to feel the question even more strongly.

In time, I would learn that I did have a calling, one that would lead me beyond the guardrails of my Catholicism and to a life different from anything I could have imagined.

The Backyard

When in the summer of 1966 others in our group prepared to travel to several islands near Jamaica before returning to the U.S., I declined to join in. I was eager to head home.

My parents' house was built on a half an acre of land. Behind the house was a flagstone terrace, and ten feet below that, a large tree rooted in a spacious well-kept lawn. On my return home I took up residence behind that tree in a chaise lounge. It was private there, even out of my parents' line of sight. That summer I spent many hours in the chaise lounge, isolating myself. Sometimes I read, sometimes I thought, sometimes I prayed; but mostly I spaced out.

My parents were concerned. "Is everything OK?" my mother would ask. Or "What's wrong?" I had no clear answer to give.

I had just come home after a year away and some friends were calling, asking to see me, but I agreed to see only a few. Again, this was so strange for me; I had always been open-hearted.

———

That fall I was scheduled to start graduate school at the Teachers College of New York's Columbia University. I had been admitted there for a two-year master's program in nursing, an idea my mother and I had discussed before I left for Jamaica. Mom was the administrative assistant to the Dean of Brandeis University Graduate School and a strong believer in the life-long value of education. She had pushed me toward an advanced degree.

I agreed with my mother's logic, but sitting on the back lawn, I knew an advanced degree in nursing was not the answer to my gnawing question. That question erupted when it came time for me to say goodbye. Facing my mother as we stood together in our kitchen on the day I was leaving for New York, I suddenly reached out, grabbed her by the shoulders, and shook her. "What am I supposed to do for God?" I cried out.

Unsurprisingly, my mother had no answer. She took in my question, stayed calm and encouraged me to just get to New York. "Somehow it will work out."

She wasn't wrong but my desperation did not let me take much comfort from her words. I left for New York, knowing I was alone in this quest, hoping I would be guided from above.

My childhood friend Margie and her fiancée Paul drove me

to New York. Paul was soon leaving for Vietnam and as he bid me a smiling farewell outside the door to my dorm, I had the feeling I might not see him again. And I didn't. A tragic casualty would bring the war close to home, especially for Margie.

3

New York

Still Questioning

New York was different from Boston, and it had a harder edge. At Boston College I was a vital part of the community, but at Teachers College I was in unknown territory. Standing in line to register at Teachers College, I felt insignificant.

As my studies at Teachers College were financed by scholarships, I needed to maintain a B+ average. This meant a lot of time studying in my postage-stamp-sized dorm room. Even so, I managed to make a few friends.

Beyond the dorm, I sought connection with my roots by attending a local Catholic Church and trying to join its choir. The ability to read music being a requirement, and my faking of such an ability on my audition being unpersuasive, I didn't make the cut.

Walking on Fifth Avenue one day that Fall I looked at the skyscrapers and asked, "What are you going to teach me?"

Later in my first semester my continuing uncertainty led me to make an appointment with the school counselor. For the first fifteen minutes he took copious notes, looked at me occasionally, and finally interrupted my pressured monologue. "I think," he said, "I will refer you to…" He sent me to a Jewish psychologist in Greenwich Village, a man perhaps better equipped to deal with the dense muddle I was presenting.

For a year I saw my therapist once or twice a week, depending on my finances. The cost was $25 per session, money which needed to come out of my scholarship funds. I cut back in other areas to continue my internal exploration.

With no agenda of his own, my therapist allowed me to speak about whatever came up. In addition to "talk therapy", my work included role playing about relationships in my family. Through this process I realized I had received an unspoken commandment growing up: "Be happy!" To comply, I had learned to suppress feelings of sadness, anger and guilt.

I had never learned to be myself.

After a year, I had learned much and felt ready to move on. The termination process brought up sweet tears and appreciative words from both my therapist and me.

My therapy was a gift. It helped me emerge from a cocoon with new abilities. I began to trust myself and listen more fully to my own inner voice.

Those capacities would soon be needed.

Farley Again

On a weekday afternoon in March of 1967, I was sitting in my dorm room when an unexpected thought suddenly arose in my mind with a directive force: "Go to the bookstore."

If I needed a book in those days, I would typically go to the nearby Teachers College bookstore. This time, however, I had the clear sense that I was to go not there, but to the more-distant undergraduate store. This struck me as unusual.

I stood up to go and then sat back down. "You have been buying books," I said to myself, "but these days you don't read them." This was true, but the internal push continued, and I finally got up and headed out. On the way, my ambivalence persisted: "Go." "Don't go." As I walked south on Broadway, perhaps halfway to the store, I almost turned around. "Why go there? There is no reason!"

But I kept walking.

Entering the bookstore, I went straight to the section on religion and philosophy. There I saw some authors whose names I recognized. Standing in an aisle surrounded by books, I casually started to browse.

Then I looked up.

"Farley?"

Since meeting him five years before I had seen Farley on several occasions. One of those was in the summer of 1964 when my parents and I happened to be having dinner at Cape Cod's Coonamessett Inn. There was Farley, waiting tables. I was happy to see him. I think the feeling was mutual.

The serendipity of that moment was now exceeded by this one. Again, meeting Farley, this time in a narrow bookstore aisle in the middle of New York City? What were the chances?

Was meeting him the reason I had felt compelled to go to this bookstore?

Farley invited me to take some time to catch-up at a grille across Broadway. Sitting across from him in a booth, I learned that he had discovered a new religious teaching which had grabbed his interest. He questioned some of its tenets, and since I was a "good Catholic" he wanted my thoughts about some of the ideas he was encountering.

The philosophy he was studying, called the Divine Principle, was based on the teachings of a Korean man named Sun

Myung Moon, later to be known as Reverend Moon.

As I learned, Reverend Moon had teachings on the purpose of life, the fall of man, divine providence, the mission of Jesus and the restoration of humanity's relationship with God.

Farley had a particular question on Reverend Moon's teaching that the crucifixion of Jesus represented not a fulfillment of Jesus' divine purpose, but a frustration of it. "What do you think of that?" he asked. Not wanting to discourage him from his new-found spiritual interest, I avoided refutation. "Well," I said, "maybe…"

When Farley told me that the teaching described the Biblical Fall of Adam and Eve as a sexual sin, I replied without hesitation, "I believe that's true."

I knew Farley had been an atheist during his years at Princeton University. Now, with his new interest in spiritual matters, I felt we had more in common. I was happy that we were having this kind of a discussion.

I also brought Farley up to date with my life. I had been writing to someone from Boston College who was currently serving as a lay missionary in Baghdad, Iraq. I avoided details, not mentioning that I saw him as a possible marriage partner. My interest reflected my desire for a mate with an orientation toward God and an interest in serving Him.

Farley and I met one more time that Spring, going for a bike ride in Central Park. I understood that thereafter he was heading to Washington D.C. where he would continue his studies of the Moon teachings in a residential center.

A Disappointed Heart

I had met Mike at Boston College, and after he left for Iraq I had been writing to him from both Jamaica and New York. In my heart I was corresponding with him because I considered him a potential marriage partner. I had not felt this way toward anyone before.

In mid-July of 1967 he returned from Baghdad. I had much anticipation about our meeting, hoping we could discuss a shared future.

That was not to be.

"Betsy," he told me as we sat in a coffee shop in suburban Boston," I have decided to return to Iraq. For two more years." He went on to say that if he were ready to marry, I would be the kind of person he would want. "But I'm not ready. I am uncertain about things. I do not want to take you through whatever I have to sort out."

My heart hit bottom and tears flowed freely. I had allowed myself to develop expectations about a future with him. I had put my romantic life on hold for this relationship, turning away others who were interested in me.

For now, those hopes were dashed.

The Ride from Hell

In that summer of 1967, I worked as a nurse at Massachusetts General Hospital, living in Cambridge. Toward summer's end, I took a Greyhound to New York to arrange for an apartment for my second year at Teachers College. On the return trip, I chatted with two young men sitting in front of me who, when they learned I planned to take a cab from the Newton Greyhound station to Cambridge, offered to drive me. As it was almost midnight, I naively accepted.

We walked through the Greyhound parking lot to an old sedan with a three-person bench. One of the young men opened the door to let me in first; I then found myself in the front seat in the middle of the two men. Soon, we were on the road.

"Hey!" I exclaimed as we entered Watertown and passed a

sign to Cambridge, "You missed the turn!" "I know a shorter way," the driver said.

I was not reassured. The further we drove, the more I realized I was in trouble. We reached streets I didn't recognize and neighborhoods with fewer lights. Coming to signs for Walpole prison, the driver turned off the road into an empty, pitch-black parking area behind the prison; he stopped the car and turned off the engine.

Was I about to die? I did not know, but I did know I was not going to give in to this impending evil. I uttered a silent prayer: "God, I will die if it is necessary. I will remain with You."

Now as the two men grabbed at me their intentions became unmistakable, and insistent. I fought off their hands, but they were not taking "No" for an answer. "Just this once!" the driver shouted as he tried to remove my blouse. "Otherwise, I will kill you!" "No way," I shouted. "I would rather die." As they both punched me and tore at my clothes, I punched back, both to the left and to the right. I kept yelling and punching. For how long, I don't know.

The one on my right was less menacing, so I focused on hitting him. "Don't you have a sister?" I screamed. "Would you treat her like this?" I also began to threaten them with lies: "My father is the police chief of Boston. He'll find you!"

Then, a sudden concession came from the one on the right: "Let's stop. There may be a few decent broads in this world."

I had been trying to get to the passenger door, and now, as the driver turned the engine on, I was pushed and pulled over the man on my right and shoved onto the pavement. The car sped away in the darkness, with its lights off. "Smart," I thought; I couldn't see the license plate number.

Shaking, I stood up and looked at a sky filled with stars, deeply grateful that I was still alive. Walking away on a narrow road, I felt a distinct intimacy with God, as though I had fought this battle with Him. "Why did you save my life?" I asked.

After walking a good distance, I came to a house with a welcoming light. Even though it was past midnight, I rang the bell. A kindly middle-aged man opened the door, took one look at my ruffled hair and dirty clothes, and invited me in. After a few moments of listening to my story, he said, "I will get my wife," and left the room.

I now looked at the fireplace mantle and noticed a picture of the family taken years before. I walked over to it and saw five young children standing between their parents. With the question of "Why?" still very much with me, I had the thought that I, too, would have five children. Then, more thoughts arose, with surprising content: I would help the family of man, I would serve in a broader context than that of the Catholic Church, and I would work with people of other nationalities and other faiths.

I had the sense that the ideas forming in my mind were coming from beyond my finite awareness. Somehow, the trauma I had just been through had opened interior doors to spiritual perception.

When the man re-appeared with his wife, I recounted at breakneck speed exactly what had happened to me. Listening quietly, empathetically, they offered me catharsis.

The police soon arrived and drove me to my parents' house. "Why didn't you call me from the bus station?" my father exclaimed vehemently. "I would gladly have come." I knew calling him would have been a better choice, and I would not wish my experience on anyone, but it had mysteriously led to a sense of God's presence and to a holy communication. How could I regret that?

I did not try to share my inner experience with my parents.

It was something I felt I should keep to myself.

It was soon time to return to New York to start my second year at Teachers College. With no specific answer to my spiritual search in view, I began to think I should just adapt to the existing culture. I had my hair frosted at the expensive Louis Guy D. Salon on Fifth Avenue, bought clothes at trendy Bergdorf Goodman and threw parties in my apartment with pizza and beer. One night I got drunk and circled the room hugging each guest: "You are a beautiful person," I repeated to each one. "The heck with worrying about what I am supposed to do for God," I thought. "Maybe this is it!"

Yet a party life was not for me. Telling people that they were beautiful was an effort at connection, but I was not connecting. That night after my guests left, I sat down at my kitchen table, put my head down on my arm, and allowed myself to feel my emptiness.

4

Unified Family

A Letter of Introduction

In October, I received an unexpected call from a woman who introduced herself as Diane, the director of the Unified Family in New York. I had heard the name of the organization, as Farley had mentioned it when we had met the previous spring. It was the group he was studying with.

Diane was calling because she had a letter for me from Farley. "Would you like to pick it up?" she asked. I was not interested in the group or in another religion, but I was lonely and wanted to see what the letter said.

Several days later, I arrived at a humble apartment a few blocks north of Times Square, where I met Diane and Wesley, an African American man who was a member of the group. After brief introductions, Diane pulled Farley's letter from a nearby bookshelf and handed it to me. Farley, I came to understand, had finally accepted the Divine Principle. His letter was succinct, offering a few words of greeting and expressing the hope that I would hear Mr. Moon's teachings. In addition to this encouragement, he emphasized that I "should not judge the people."

When I finished the letter, Diane asked me if I would like to hear an introductory lecture. Knowing that Farley had been impressed by the teachings, and that they seemed to have had a good effect on his life, I consented.

It was a fateful decision.

Beginning weekly visits to the Unified Family center, I went on to hear the complete series of lectures on the Divine Principle. I also met more members, including Helen, a young woman who was living in the center.

Certain aspects of the teachings appealed to me. For example, I much liked the Divine Principle concept of a "God-centered" marriage; I very much believed in that. I also liked the emphasis on sexual abstinence before marriage; even though my values were slowly being worn down by my graduate school culture, I still shared this ideal. I already believed it was what God intended.

I was less sure about other teachings, including the idea that Jesus' original mission was to become the second Adam, take a bride who was to be the second Eve, and restore the failure of the first Adam.

On one occasion, during a discussion with Diane and others on marriage, I suddenly connected my serendipitous meetings with Farley to the high ideal of marriage expressed in the teaching. "Oh!" I burst out." Maybe I have been led here because I'm supposed to marry Farley Jones!"

My exclamation was met with silence. Dating and pairing off just didn't happen in the group, and such matters were not discussed.

But I'm a Good Catholic!

During the process of studying with Unified Family members, a persistent question slowly began to present itself: "Is this where God is leading me? Could this be my calling?"

If I was being led to this group, it was producing an inner conflict.

I had no interest leaving the Catholic Church or in joining a new religion.

Throughout my relatively short life, I had questions and periods of uncertainty about my purpose in life, but never about being a member of the Catholic faith. I had gone to a Catholic grammar school, high school, and college. I had attended Mass every Sunday when I was growing up, attended noon Mass at Boston College chapel several days a week for four years, and attended Mass regularly at Columbia. I had searched inwardly, prayed, and read theological works that sustained me through spiritually challenging times. In my life as a Catholic, Jesus was a living presence.

I had also flourished in the social and cultural environment of my Catholic faith. After serving as president of Sodality in high school, I had become the head of student government in my senior year at the Boston College School of Nursing. At my college graduation, I had received a standing ovation from my classmates for an award I was given. My sister was a nun, and my parents were devoted Catholics. My closest friends were Catholic. My faith had given me confidence, community, and a sense of belonging. I was deeply and happily embedded in my Catholic cocoon.

Being Catholic was not something I did, it was who I was.

So why was I looking elsewhere? Why was I spending time with this unknown, virtually invisible little group? This was not the kind of community I would ever choose to join.

One day, I asked Diane a pointed question: "If this is a new revelation, why isn't it coming from the Pope?"

This was one of my many questions, and I asked some of them with no little arrogance. Diane handled them, and me, with gentleness and patience.

A Compelling Question

One of the reasons I continued studying lay with the claim that emerged from the conclusion of the Divine Principle teachings. The claim was that Reverend Moon was the chosen successor to Jesus. In him, the long-awaited Second Coming of Christ was being fulfilled.

According to the Divine Principle, Adam was to be the true father of humankind, Eve the true mother. Together they were to give birth to a family which in its varying relationships was to come to embody God's love. This first family was to spread to a tribe, clan, society, nation and world, with each level substantiating the expansion of God's love on earth. This was the divine ideal. This was to be the Kingdom of God.

Because of the Fall, the ideal was not realized. Millenia later, Jesus came as the second Adam to take a bride as the second Eve; together they were to realize the original Divine purpose. Because Jesus was rejected, the ideal was, again, not realized.

Now Sun Myung Moon had in God's ongoing providence come as the third Adam. Born in 1920, he married Hak Ja Han in 1960. The ceremony was understood to be the fulfillment of the Book of Revelation promise of the Marriage Supper of the Lamb. In the marriage of the Moon couple and in their subsequent mission, the fall of Adam and Eve had been reversed. For the first time in history, True Parents for humankind had emerged, restoring the position of the false parents of Genesis.

These were radical claims; for some reason I felt I could not ignore them.

But was I to believe?

Diane had given me a book, *The Divine Principle*, written by Young Oon Kim, the first missionary to bring the teachings to the United States. There was much in it that appealed to me but studying it one day in my dorm room, my deep uncertainty surfaced. I stood up, flung the book against the wall, and shouted "How do I know if you are true?"

I didn't know, and I didn't see how I could ever know for sure.

But a mystical process was quietly at work. I was being drawn.

I said yes when Diane invited me to join Helen and her on a weekend trip to visit the group's national headquarters, which was then in Washington, D.C.

At the Washington center, I met Young Oon Kim, called "Miss Kim," by the members. She had done graduate work at the University of Toronto and had been a professor of New Testament Studies at the prestigious Ewha Women's University in Seoul, Korea. Fluent in English, passionate about God and gifted with a loving spirit, she had established Unified Family centers throughout the United States in the eight years since her arrival on the West Coast.

During the weekend, I ventured to push my own envelope: "Miss Kim," I said, "how would I grow my faith in the Divine Principle? "Well," she answered after a moment, "if you have only two percent faith, then act on it. It will grow to four percent. If you have only four percent faith, act on that, and it will become eight percent."

Two percent faith? Four percent? Yes, that was probably about where I was.

The Unified Family headquarters at 1907 S Street, Northwest, was in a brick rowhouse that provided a communal center for about fifteen members, all living as spiritual brothers and sisters. Their number included Farley. In a brief conversation with me, he asserted his conviction in the group's teachings.

I was still unsure of that intellectually, but emotionally, something was underway. Standing with several members Sunday evening as I started to depart, I suddenly experienced what felt like a deep wave of love flowing through them toward me and into me. In this love, I felt I was coming home. As I said goodbye to each person, tears filled my eyes.

I had wanted to maintain a neutral stance during the weekend, but my tears betrayed me.

God was reaching me through my heart.

Things were moving fast for me and for the New York Unified Family members. It was still autumn when the lease on their apartment expired, and Diane and Helen squeezed in with Wesley and his family in their Brooklyn home. I continued to visit them there.

One day, I was thinking of them when I happened to close my eyes. The image of a map of New York City emerged in my mind, showing that a light in Manhattan had moved out to Brooklyn. "Wow!" I thought. "Does this group represent a kind of light?"

It was doing that, at least for me.

In fact, Brooklyn would be the site of a major pivot.

The Answer

One Saturday in November, Diane invited me to join the group in an evening prayer meeting and sleep-over at Wesley's house to avoid the long commute back to my apartment.

I arrived with my toothbrush, pajamas, and, to my surprise,

an unusual feeling of anticipation.

That night, in Wesley's small living room, seven participants sat in a circle, singing, studying the Divine Principle, discussing questions, and offering prayer. The meeting lasted about an hour, with Diane uttering a heartfelt closing prayer. As she prayed, I had a striking experience: from deep within, I suddenly heard a clear, unmistakable message, my own personal revelation about the Divine Principle: "Betsy, it's true."

With this, my major conflicts dissolved. I felt I could and should move forward with this new teaching, this new community, and this new faith.

Later that night, I asked Diane for a membership application. Sitting at Wesley's dining room table, I quickly read and signed it in front of Diane and Helen. As I handed it back to Diane, Helen jokingly said, "You've just signed your life away."

That comment would prove to be not far from the truth.

Joining the Unified Family, accepting its teachings and aligning myself with Reverend Moon's mission was the beginning of the end of my long search for what God wanted me to do. My decision opened the door to the life I believe God was prompting me toward all along.

Moving in that direction would not be simple, and life ahead would test my decision.

Culture Clash

Diane and Helen were looking for a new apartment in Manhattan, and I felt I should live with them. Since my apartment was in a desirable location on West 91st Street at Riverside

Drive, I invited them to move in with me.

With a blackboard now nailed on the center of the living room wall, my apartment became the Unified Family Center of New York. With my two new spiritual sisters, I began to live as a member of a small spiritual community and to participate in Center activities.

The clarity I had felt at the prayer meeting in Brooklyn receded, however, and I soon developed mixed feelings. One day I told Diane that if I stopped believing in this new faith, she and Helen could have the apartment, and I would just move on.

Diane and Helen had jobs during the day and "witnessed" during the evenings and on weekends. On many Saturdays, they sold cosmetics door to door for added income. On Sundays, Diane led a worship service where she stood in front of Helen and me in our living room, conducted us in singing hymns, and offered a prepared sermon. Afterward, we often went to the coffee hour at different churches to meet people we could invite to the Center to hear the Divine Principle.

I was a busy student, and my participation was limited, but studies were not my only limitation. In particular, I had no heart for the cosmetics' sales activities. I hit the streets with Diane and Helen a few times, going door-to-door in Manhattan. Contradicting the essential purpose of the work, if a customer liked a product but couldn't afford it, I would sometimes just give it away.

To say that all this was new and different is an understatement. This was not a life I knew, and not a life I felt comfortable with.

Prior to becoming the New York Center leader, Diane had spent six months living in a Unified Family Center in Japan. When she or Helen offered me or a guest a cup of tea, it was done with all the trappings of a Japanese tea ceremony. With the tea prepared, the server wrapped both hands around the cup, and the cup was passed with a slight bow to its recipient, ever so slowly, ever so respectfully. I could see the beauty in the practice, but it also seemed very strange. "We're not Japanese." I thought.

It helped that I could tease them and laugh with them about it.

Despite my resistance to some aspects of center life, I remembered Miss Kim's two percent-four percent guidance, so I began to act on my small grain of faith. I invited a few of my fellow master's degree classmates to my apartment. Observing the new blackboard in the living room and learning of my membership evoked a common reaction: "I can't believe you are doing this."

I had previously dated one person who stopped by. After I shared what I had learned, he said as he left, "Well, I don't know if I should kiss you goodbye or ask for your blessing."

Overall, acting on my two percent wasn't exactly doing the trick. In fact, I felt my life had become too restricted. This was not at all what I thought I should be doing as a student at Columbia. I began to feel like bowing out.

My internal tensions came to a head one night over the issue of the Center menu. I had grown up with meat and potatoes as staples, but since Diane had established a partially Asian culture within the Center, these were rare commodities, and I was frustrated. "What's wrong with a hamburger?" I asked Diane as we stood one night in the kitchen. Apparently offended by the tone of my question, she answered sharply, "Nothing's wrong with hamburger. Fish and vegetables are just better choices."

"You know, Diane," I retorted, "for me, this life is just so narrow. Perhaps it's time for me to move out."

I stomped out of the apartment, headed up 91st Street to Broadway. Walking down Broadway, I came to a movie theater, and decided to buy a ticket. "Maybe a movie will calm me down."

I knew nothing about the movie I was about to see except that it was in French and had subtitles. I purposefully sat in the front of the theater where I could get the greatest impact.

If ever a movie was R rated, this was it. Watching the free sex scenes made me think of the human condition. I felt sad that people could be so misled as to what would bring them happiness.

Not happy with what I was watching, I nevertheless soon learned that my choice had not been in error. Part-way through the movie, a surprising subtitle ran across the bottom of the screen, stunning me: "A religion that does not make you suffer will have no meaning in your life."

The idea hit me like a lightning bolt. This new faith was certainly causing me to suffer, but could such suffering lead me to a more meaningful life?

I decided to turn back, to live with my resistance and ambivalence, and to have faith that greater clarity would come.

I was glad that I had expressed my frustration to Diane, but relieved to return with greater acceptance in my heart.

I started to tell a few more people about the Divine Principle and prepared to teach a small section of it called "The Mission of Jesus." On the day my first student arrived, I stood in front of him with a knotted stomach as I began to write on the blackboard.

This was my dilemma: I had come to accept the Divine Principle ideas about Jesus' mission, but to teach it to someone else was at that point a step too far.

In fact, I remained torn in my relationship with Jesus. I accepted that Reverend Moon had come as his successor, but I had a deep loyalty to Jesus and a great love for him. I could not simply turn that off. Did I have to choose between them?

In the winter of 1968, several months after I had joined, a Korean named Won Pil Kim, a warm-hearted man recognized as Reverend Moon's first disciple, visited our small New York center. He could not have known about my continuing inner conflict, but during a talk he gave us one night, he spoke directly to it.

That night, Mr. Kim described Reverend Moon's heart toward Jesus.

He spoke through tears.

I came to learn Reverend Moon's relationship with Jesus was one of depth and devotion. Reverend Moon knew, as I explain below, that Jesus had called him to his mission, knew that he stood on Jesus' sacrificial foundation and, most importantly, knew of and had embraced Jesus' suffering heart.

Mr. Kim's sincerity was apparent. Listening to him, I grasped that Reverend Moon and Jesus were in some mystical way one. There was no separation between them, in heart and in mission. It was an insight that spoke to my heart.

By the end of Mr. Kim's talk, my conflict was gone.

A Friend in Faith

Diane and Helen were patient, empathetic and loving, but in those early days I felt something missing. Diane had been a Quaker, and Helen, broadly Protestant. I longed for a companion in this small community who shared my Catholic roots.

Walking through the Teachers' College dorm one evening, I

encountered a Catholic nun whom I had met once before. Sister Mary Eudes Klein was in the Education Department's doctoral program, and she was president of the student government at Teachers College. She was slight in stature but strong in spirit, and her face exuded light. When I stopped by her room that night, she began to share freely about herself and then asked me how I was doing. "Do you really want to know?" I asked, and eagerly told her about my new understanding.

Sister Mary said nothing to stop me, so I poured out the central ideas of the Divine Principle, proceeding from the beginning to the conclusion.

To my great surprise, she expressed interest. "Hmm. Do you think this is related to the Parousia?" she asked. Knowing the term referred to the Second Coming of Christ, I quietly murmured "I think so."

For the next six months, Sister Mary studied the teachings at our center, bringing her Bible to most sessions to compare its teachings with those of the Divine Principle. Finding much in the teachings that resonated with her, she decided to visit the Washington headquarters where she could meet Miss Kim.

Her experience in Washington reinforced her conviction that she also was being called to this new work. Despite warnings from authorities within her religious order, she made the dramatic decision to join our small group in New York. She was now no longer Sister Mary Eudes Klein but Therese, a dear spiritual sister.

It was a huge fulfillment of an earnest hope. Therese's joining offered me great support, a support that has continued throughout my life.

———

Toward the end of my spring semester at Teachers College, I called Miss Kim, asking if I could spend the summer in

Washington. I felt I needed more spiritual nurturing than the New York center could provide, and I thought the larger community of members in Washington would provide that. Miss Kim invited me to come as soon as school finished.

My stay in Washington would be brief.

5

Deepening

*"I have come home at last! This is my real country!
I belong here. This is the land I have been looking
for all my life, though I never knew it till now...Come
further up, come further in!"*
—C.S. Lewis, Narnia Chronicles, The Last Battle

Starting at the Bottom

Wrapping up the semester at Columbia, I happily headed to the Unified Family National Headquarters.

After the 1968 assassination of Dr. Martin Luther King, rioting near the headquarters had caused the community, with about twenty members, to move to McLean, Virginia. There another Korean missionary owned a home. Arriving at the modern split-level house, I found a warm welcome: "Hi Betsy. I am glad you're here!" Similar greetings echoed from all the members.

In general, the community had a light, happy spirit, the likely product of Miss Kim's presence and the members' working together for a common ideal.

Most members had full time jobs, though some were students, and some had roles within the group that required them to spend their days in the Center.

Meeting with Miss Kim soon after my arrival, I told her more about why I had come. I wanted to make progress on this new path, and I thought time in a larger community would help. She listened attentively and then offered me a job. "Would you be responsible for cleaning the toilets?" she asked. "Huh? Clean toilets?" I thought to myself. Quickly overcoming my ambivalence, I told her I would be happy to do it.

In retrospect, I saw the wisdom of her request. She had given me a humble position where I could serve everyone. This role helped me quickly feel like an integral part of the community.

I was at home.

Miss Kim also suggested that I have a weekly study session with Philip, the center leader and then president of the organization. Wary of having too much focus on me, I was relieved that another new member, George, was to study with us.

The initial topic of our study was the existence of the spirit world. George also had a Catholic background, so the notion of a spiritual realm was familiar to both of us, but the Divine Principle view was quite developed. Philip added details and examples, including some based on his own spiritual experiences. It was a lot to take in. Sometimes George and I exchanged quick glances; it was reassuring to know I was not alone in trying to absorb so much otherworldly information.

Again, Miss Kim knew what she was doing. Being part of the study group helped me get to know George and Philip better and learn more about the teachings. I was feeling more and more a part of life at the Center.

Trusted

Formal study with Philip and an "essential service" job, along with routine activities of cooking, washing up, witnessing, lectures, and prayer meetings, were helping me grow some spiritual muscle. Becoming attuned to this new way of life, I was gaining confidence that I could contribute to the growth of Reverend Moon's mission.

About two weeks after I arrived, Miss Kim received a letter from the Unified Family group in Berkeley, California. The leader there had a request: since there were only two male members, and no females, could Miss Kim send a "sister" to help?

Sitting in the bright, spacious living room of the McLean house, Miss Kim read the letter out loud to a small group of us and turned toward me: "Betsy, would you be willing to go?"

She had clearly given some thought to the request.

Although I was expecting to stay at headquarters all summer, and knew I was still a spiritual novice, I didn't hesitate: "Yes, I will go."

After two weeks, I had received what I needed. I came to the headquarters to be helped, but now I would be a helper. I had arrived trusting, and now I was being trusted.

I was inspired.

Farley had gone to Berkeley the preceding fall, so I already knew one of the two members there. The other person, Miss Kim explained, was Edwin, a full time doctoral student in economics at the University of California. Edwin had to focus on his studies, and Farley needed help with witnessing and teaching.

Before I left, Miss Kim gave me three instructions: I was to find three young women, teaching them the Divine Principle and how to be sisterly with the brothers, I was to share the teaching practices used at the headquarters, and I was to avoid falling in love with either Edwin or Farley.

I arrived in Berkeley with these instructions, an eager spirit, and an Adele Davis cookbook.

I was ready!

Berkeley Blessings

The center in Berkeley was in a three-bedroom flat located on the second and third floors of a home on Berkeley's Milvia Street, only a few blocks from the University of California campus.

I was welcomed not only by Edwin and Farley but also by the warm sunshine, blue skies, and pleasant climate of northern California.

Indonesian by birth, Chinese by ancestry and in his early forties, Edwin possessed smiling eyes, a moderate build, and a calm presence. He had joined the Unified Family some four years earlier. During my eight-week Berkeley adventure, I would come to appreciate his stable nature and clear faith. Farley's educational and religious background was like mine, and his presence reassured me about the choices I was making. He became a role model in our shared spiritual work in Berkeley: teaching the Divine Principle and guiding new students.

Believing I could contribute positively to the Berkeley mission, I was happy to be there.

My experience would not be all peaches and cream. Miss Kim had asked me to be a model for how teaching was done at the headquarters, and I was a bit quick with that agenda. This evoked a less-than-positive response from Edwin and Farley, but a frank airing of differences helped us all overcome a difficult patch.

Farley and I witnessed to students on the Berkeley campus

and to non-students on the Berkeley streets. Seekers of all types started to visit the center for lectures, discussions, and frequent dinners. Farley was a busy teacher of the Divine Principle, and Edwin offered wise counsel for those interested in further study. As a novice mentor, I enjoyed welcoming and guiding new people.

I was particularly invested in introducing young residents of the liberal Berkeley culture to the Divine Principle emphasis on sexual abstinence before marriage. I presented the practice as an important cornerstone for a more spiritually oriented and less complicated marriage.

I also enjoyed trying new recipes and receiving appreciative responses from our guests.

Growing Together

In the next weeks, some students accepted the Principle and moved into the center. Roger was a remarkably open-hearted young man in his early twenties, a friend of someone I had met. More than ready to hear the teaching, he quickly joined. Learning of Roger's decision, Jeff, who had been studying for several months, reversed a decision to enroll in a Los Angeles Bible college and moved in.

Linda was a Cal. Berkeley student working as a nurse's aide at a local hospital where I had taken a position, and she responded to my invitation. A devout Catholic, she nevertheless found new light in the Divine Principle. After taking up residence with us, she invited several of her friends, and some of them joined.

What did these young people find? Responses were as different as the people were, but the logic of the Principle, its vision of God-centered marriage as the basis for a transformed world, and the warmth of a spiritual community were major factors. They also responded to our sincere faith in what we were teaching.

Whatever the reasons, the Unified Family in Berkeley started to grow.

The summer went quickly and the time for me to return to Columbia arrived. With many young seekers studying the Principle, I felt my presence in Berkeley was needed, but I knew I had only one semester to go, my parents had expectations of me, and if I did not return, I would lose my scholarship. Considering everything, I thought I should complete my studies.

But I was torn.

I decided to consult with Miss Kim. "Come back," she said. "I will send someone in your place." That reassured me.

In Berkeley, I grew in confidence as a teacher and mentor. I saw the power this teaching had to make positive changes in others' lives, and I left feeling inspired.

Further, I had developed close bonds with Edwin and Farley. I had long held the hope of marrying someone who could be a partner in serving God and carrying on spiritual work. Membership in the Unified Family meant marrying within it, and my experience with these two spiritual brothers reassured me that there were men in the group with whom I could fulfill this ideal. It was a welcome realization to take from that summer.

In late August, I took my leave and flew back to New York.

Returning to Columbia University in September 1968 for my last semester, I found my heart was not in academic work. I put a minimum number of hours into my studies and focused on the work of the New York Center.

At the end of the semester, I was surprised to discover that my grades were the same or better than they had been before.

In December, I learned that Reverend and Mrs. Moon were coming to Washington D.C. in late January. Having finished my academic program, I decided I would volunteer my services to help with the Moons' visit. Miss Kim welcomed my offer and later asked me to assist another sister in meal preparation for the Moon party. Inexperienced in preparing Korean food, we were nervous. "Don't worry," Miss Kim said. "They like tuna fish."

6

Honored Guests

*The Kingdom of Heaven is meant not for individuals,
but for the family: grandparents, parents, and children, bound together in love.*

—Sun Myung Moon

Marriage is the only sacrament in Reverend Moon's teaching, and it is the essential focus of his mission. For him,
the love that is to unfold in marriage and in the family is an
expression of divine love; the true family is the central purpose
of God's creation.

At that time, Reverend Moon developed his mission by
arranging matches for his followers and blessing them in
marriage.

He was coming to the U.S. to match and bless couples for
the first time from within the American membership. Unified Family members who were potential marriage candidates
were on pins and needles.

The Meeting

In late January 1969, the itinerary for the Moons and their
party took them first to San Francisco and then to Washington.

We were ready to receive them.

The Unified Family in Washington had recently purchased a large Victorian house on Upshur Street Northwest, to serve as its national headquarters. The building had previously served as the Libyan Embassy. It would now host the Moons' visit.

The front door of Upshur House, as it came to be called, opened into a broad hallway perhaps twelve feet across, covered with an emerald-green carpet. Prior to their arrival, Washington members lined up on either side of the hallway, waiting to greet the Moons with applause as they came through the front door.

Standing and waiting in the line with others, I wondered what they would be like.

Upon entering and receiving our welcome, the Moons started to make their way down the lines of members, warmly greeting each person and shaking hands.

When he came to me, Reverend Moon looked me in the eye and asked, "Where are your ancestors from?" "Ireland," I said, relieved by the simplicity of the question. "Oh! Irishee!" he replied with a warm, broad grin. He seemed pleased to meet someone of Irish descent, perhaps the first such person he had met. My gleeful reply, "Yes!" reflected my pride in my heritage.

It was a special moment, one that revealed him to me as a man of deep heart. I felt an immediate personal connection.

The couple's warm greeting to each of us brought welcome relief. This heralded couple did not disappoint. They seemed to be who I had hoped they would be.

Bonding

Just off the broad center hallway on the main floor of Upshur House were two large meeting rooms. The room nearest the building front became the site for the next phase of our welcome: entertainment.

Sometime before the Moons' arrival, I had been asked to join a small group assigned to prepare the entertainment. We would open with "Let's Move America!" a song written by a Los Angeles church leader, and then there would be individual and small group performances of songs and poetry. Since the Moons' main purpose for this visit was to match and marry couples, we created a skit acting out the process. Two members played the role of the Moons, and others took on the roles of newly matched couples who were awkwardly trying to relate to each other.

Before our show began, our primary audience gathered in the front of the room, sitting in separate chairs, surrounded by Korean church leaders, including Miss Kim, Mr. Eu (the Korean church president), and Mrs. Choi, the Moons' personal assistant and translator.

The Moons were an attractive couple. Then approaching fifty, Reverend Moon was a handsome, solidly built, bright-spirited man with an expressive face and deep-set eyes. Mrs. Moon was much younger, in her late twenties, with a quietly beautiful face and black hair pulled into a bun. In undertaking a world mission tour to visit the United States and Europe, they had left eight children behind in Korea.

I am sure they missed their family, but they were fully present with us, embracing us as their spiritual family. They smiled, laughed, and clapped as members offered their best efforts to entertain them. Within a few minutes of the beginning of the comedic skit we had planned and taking in the awkward antics of those playing the newly matched couples, the Moons began to howl with laughter.

Our efforts seemed to make them feel welcome.

At the end of our night's performances, they stood up and offered a heartfelt rendition of a traditional Korean anthem. It was their way of giving something back

The Moon's, Miss Kim, and other visitors took their meals sometimes in a room on the main floor of Upshur House and sometimes in the basement dining room with Center members. One morning, as I was helping serve them breakfast in the basement, I was suddenly addressed by Miss Kim: " Betsy, wait. I will tell them about Berkeley." She then proceeded to give a report in Korean; I heard the names of Edwin, Farley, and Betsy mentioned several times.

I stood there awkwardly for several minutes as Reverend Moon nodded his head and smiled, seeming to take great interest in Miss Kim's report. He interrupted several times to ask questions and make comments that were translated for me. Miss Kim also asked me to share a few words, which I was happy to do, especially describing my excitement over new members joining. Later Miss Kim told me Reverend Moon was pleased to hear our report.

The Matching

Several days later, Miss Kim called me to a room that served as the Upshur House office, asking me to sit at the desk with her. She wanted help in making a list of members who had been active for three years in the Unified Family movement. I understood the names on the list would be those considered eligible for Reverend Moon's matching. "This is such an important list," I thought to myself. The futures of people I knew depended on it.

Miss Kim held a typewritten list of all the Unified Family members in the U.S.; it was from this list that she selected the names of eligible marriage candidates and dictated them to me.

I wrote each name very carefully and legibly.

The list completed, Miss Kim surprised me by saying, "Betsy, put your name on the list." "Miss Kim," I replied, "I've been a member only for a year and a half." "It's OK," she said, and referring to another fairly new member, added "Also put down Vivien's name."

I felt more than nervous, as I thought I was not ready for marriage.

Still, I complied with Miss Kim's directive. Putting my name on the list, I thought, "OK. I will see what happens."

A few days later, as I was scrambling eggs on the basement kitchen stove, Miss Kim approached me. Following up on our earlier conversation, she quietly asked me what I thought about three brothers, mentioning each of their names. Farley was one of them.

Knowing that my name was on the list, I was relieved that my preferences were being considered.

I shared some brief thoughts before she revealed that she had already spoken to each of the three, and she proceeded to tell me, quoting each one, what they thought about me.

I remember several positive comments from two of the men, but there was a more muted response from Farley. He had apparently said that he felt he had "a good rapport" with me. Realizing from this conversation that I was now unexpectedly facing a serious situation, I asked for time: "Miss Kim, can I pray about this tonight?" "OK," she replied.

I devoted that night to prayerful reflection over the three

possibilities. I decided that two of them had the best balance of attributes to complement my own. I was happy I could feel comfortable with two. I had kept my heart open.

The following morning, I again met Miss Kim in the kitchen, and she asked about my preferences. Knowing that in the culture of our group, one was not to be too attached to a particular choice, my first response was that I could be flexible with either one of the two I named.

Miss Kim pushed further. "But which one do you prefer?" "Farley," I replied. She smiled, said nothing, and headed back upstairs. I think she was happy to get a clear answer, an answer I was happy to give.

I was amazed by the role Miss Kim was playing. She was sensitively trying to understand each person's heart and provide useful input to Reverend Moon in this delicate process.

Over the next couple of days, I heard about matches that were being made. At one point I bumped into Linna, a schoolteacher from Virginia perhaps three years older than I. I knew she had been matched, so I asked, "How did it go? What happened?"

Linna explained that she had been matched with Carl, a smart, funny, and somewhat intense Oregonian who was a resident of the Washington center. Carl had been invited to Reverend and Mrs. Moon's living room on the second floor, and possibilities had been discussed with him. Then Linna had been called into the same room, and after some preliminary discussion, Reverend Moon had asked her, "What about Carl?" "I had never thought of Carl," Linna told me, blushing, "but I said, 'Carl? Why, yes!' and I felt happy to say it."

I felt proud of Linna, a woman who had extended herself to someone quite different from her.

I would soon learn that my two possibilities other than Farley had evaporated. Both had, in my view, been wonderfully matched to others. For the moment, my options were down to one.

As information about matches between various members began to circulate, I continued to wonder about my own situation. Perhaps a day or two after our last conversation, Miss Kim pulled me aside and provided the answer: "Farley feels he is too young to participate in this Blessing. He wants to wait."

I had developed a willingness to participate on this occasion, but her information brought some relief. I needed more time as well.

Waiting felt right to me, but my feelings about marriage had been stirred up. I didn't know when the next marriage Blessing would take place and the question of "who" was huge. At twenty-seven, I could admit to myself that I was eagerly looking forward to answers.

The basement dining room in Upshur House was at the end of a brightly lit hallway. Walking down that hallway toward the dining room one morning after the matchings, I saw Reverend Moon coming the other way. He raised his hand to stop me. "Betsy," he said with a loving gaze, "your time is next time."

I was glad to know I was still being thought of.

Blessing 1969

By mid-February, six newly matched couples and seven previously married couples had been selected for the marriage

Blessing. The date was set for February 28, and the place would be the large front room on the main floor of Upshur House.

Over eighty people, including members, parents, and guests from outlying states began arriving to help with preparations, be in the ceremony, or just attend it. Sewing machines were running in the basement, turning yards and yards of material into white robes for the thirteen couples. The whole house was abuzz with small groups sewing, preparing flowers and decorations, rehearsing congratulatory songs, and planning a celebratory meal.

On the day of the Blessing, at the appointed time, Reverend and Mrs. Moon, in white robes with gold trim, led the procession into the room to a tune requested by Mrs. Moon: "I Dream of Jeanie With the Light Brown Hair." After they took their positions, the thirteen white-robed couples walked in while the traditional Wedding March played. Before the ceremony began, a small choir sang, "On a Clear Day, You Can See Forever."

This was not an ordinary wedding. These thirteen couples were dedicating their lives to God, to each other, and to spiritual missions intended to benefit the world.

Six of these couples were newly matched. How would their marriages develop? No one knew, but with their dedication and faith, I thought they would be equal to whatever challenges arose.

The Moons took their place in front of a beautiful teal, gold, and white banner hanging on the wall behind them. After Miss Kim offered an opening prayer, Reverend Moon asked the couples to recite a series of vows, sprinkled them with holy water and offered a heartfelt prayer in Korean. He and Mrs. Moon then proclaimed each couple to be man and wife.

That evening, couples, members, and guests gathered for

entertainment, and Reverend Moon asked each couple to sing. Dressed in their best, with shy giggles, the couples offered their first joint performances. Edwin, from Indonesia, and Marie, from the U.S. sang a well-known Christian hymn, "In Christ There is No East or West."

At the end of the evening, Reverend Moon, now in a suit, and Mrs. Moon, in a teal Korean "chimachoguri," also offered a song.

In Edwin and Marie's performance, I saw the beauty of a couple from different nations bonding with God at the center, offering a vision of a world coming closer together.

In the Moons' performance, noticing their fond looks while they sang a robust Korean song, I saw a model of the kind of marriage I wanted to have.

In this entire happy, holy experience, I felt I was getting a taste of Heaven.

A day or two later, as I was leaving Upshur House walking toward its front door, an older Korean lady, one with supposed psychic abilities but no specific church authority, approached me. "Farley Jones will be your mate," she whispered.

Well, that was uncertain. Miss Kim had already cautioned me with reference to a future Blessing: "We can't be sure who will be available next time," she said. I knew I needed to keep an open heart.

7

Engagement

Center Director

Now part of a newly matched couple, Diane would soon be moving to join her husband in Philadelphia. Miss Kim asked me to take over the leadership in New York.

Being the director of the New York Unified Family was not the only job awaiting me in New York. Now possessing a master's degree in psychiatric nursing, I had been offered work as a nurse clinician at Manhattan's Metropolitan Hospital, a role my supervisor explained would involve being a model in giving patient care on unit 13N. That unit was a locked psychiatric ward where there had been several "incidents and codes," sometimes violent actions by unstable patients. My role was to help reduce the number of such events.

I was paid ten thousand dollars a year for my service, a decent salary in those days. Needing to support myself and wanting to help support the church center, I welcomed the income.

To take care of patients at Metropolitan Hospital, I had much help from a supervisor. To take care of the New York center,

I had much help from Barbara, an older member who proved to be a warm friend and great resource. She was spirited, kind and, making up for a deficiency of mine, an excellent Divine Principle lecturer.

My strength was in my ability to unify what became a diverse group of personalities in the Center.

In addition to Barbara and me, our members came to include Maria, originally from Czechoslovakia, and Nanette, a student at New York's Parsons School of Design. They were both good at witnessing. Then came Gil, an artist who asked if he could move in even before finishing the lectures. David, from a wealthy Jewish family, wanted to move in, too, but asked if his tailor could come to measure the windows for matching curtains and bedspreads. Most members lived simply, but not David. We gave him his own room.

We grew to have eight members, living, witnessing, teaching, and worshiping together. Step-by-step, we continued to attract new people.

With our apartment filled to the brim, I asked Nanette to open a small satellite center near Columbia. She creatively developed a type of coffee house in a small apartment, and more people began studying.

I was very gratified to see our family growing.

An Airmail Letter

On a weekend in April 1970, I traveled with the other New York members to the Washington D.C. headquarters to join in the celebration of a Unified Family holiday called Parents Day. The weekend would be characterized by elaborate meals, entertainment, Sunday worship service, and opportunities to catch up with members from other cities along the East Coast.

It would also include a significant personal moment.

Four months earlier, in December 1969, Miss Kim had asked Farley to become the new president of the Unified Family in the U.S. He had since moved to Washington, where I would now see him and speak with him for the first time since I left Berkeley.

Soon after Farley's arrival in Washington, Miss Kim had returned to Korea for a visit. She periodically corresponded with him via airmail letters from Korea.

Late Saturday morning, while I was standing in the first-floor hallway, Farley approached me and asked me to go with him to his office, a postage-stamp sized room on the second floor. I followed him upstairs.

Once in the office, Farley asked me to sit down in the only chair and explained that he had received, that morning, an airmail letter from Miss Kim. "I would like you to read it," he said, before handing it to me. Saying nothing more, he walked out and closed the door behind him.

I opened the blue airmail letter and read an explanation by Miss Kim that the next marriage Blessing would be held the coming October, that it would take place in Korea, that it would be international in scope, and that couples from America would be invited.

My eyes opened wide as I read, and reread, the next sentence: It was a question for Farley: "Why don't you and Betsy come over?"

There it was. Miss Kim was proposing that Farley and I come to Korea as a matched couple.

The question that had been deeply lingering in my heart was now answered.

Sitting quietly in that small room, I thanked God for this amazing resolution. A few minutes later, Farley opened the door and came back in. "What do you think of that idea?" he asked, his face radiating a happy warmth. Smiling with my whole heart, I responded "I think it's a good idea." "So do I," I heard in response.

We spoke for a few more moments and then returned to the weekend celebrations with what was, for the moment, a precious secret.

⁓

Years earlier, when I was at Boston College, a conversation with my father proved prescient. By that time, I had dated three young men, but nothing had really clicked. "Betsy," my father said, "love is simple. You just fall in love and that's it." "No," I thought. "I want a marriage that God is part of."

I was about to get what I had long hoped for.

My Parents

"Really?" my startled mother asked. "Who?"

I had previously told my parents that I had joined the Unified Family and that I was likely to marry someone from the group, but I had never mentioned names or dates, and my news on the phone that day came as a surprise.

"Do you remember Farley Jones who dated my friend Carol?"

Yes, they remembered him. He had visited our home one time with Carol, and my parents thought they made a nice couple.

I went on to explain that Farley was also a Unified Family member and reassured my devout parents, especially my mother, that Farley also had a Catholic background. At the end of the conversation, they proposed that they would come to meet us in Washington D.C.

⁓

In early May 1970, my parents flew from Boston to meet Farley and me at Upshur House.

My mother had a request.

With the four of us sitting together on Saturday afternoon in a smaller room off the Upshur House hallway, she suddenly posed a question that revealed a real concern. "So, could you be married in a Catholic church prior to the wedding in Korea?" The question took both Farley and me aback. Not knowing what to say, we deferred an answer. That night Farley had a dream that he interpreted to mean that we should hold tight to the wedding in Korea as our main spiritual ceremony.

The next day, I told my parents our decision. It was a tense moment. In the past, I had generally listened to my parents and complied with what they wanted. For the first time, I was taking a stance against their wishes on a major issue, aligning myself with my new fiancé. It felt both odd and painful, especially for me in relation to my mother.

At the same time, Farley and I were making our first joint decision as an engaged couple, and that felt good.

To relieve the tension, I suggested an alternative: "After we return, how about a wedding reception in Boston?" The idea did not address my mother's religious concern, but it affirmed our connectedness and seemed to help.

I later heard that soon after my parents returned home, my mother took a copy of the Divine Principle to a local priest, Father Byrne. She asked him to read it and let her know if he thought that her daughter Betsy "would be married in the eyes of God."

Apparently, Father Byrne thought I would be, and so told my mother.

Many years later when Father Byrne presided at my father's funeral, I took the occasion to thank him for the gracious reassurance he had offered my mother.

Farley's Parents

In the weeks following my parents' visit, I met Farley's parents separately, as they were divorced. With Farley's father being a well-respected lawyer and his mother descended from a real estate magnate, I approached these meetings with a clear awareness of our different socio-economic backgrounds. I met Farley's mother at Manhattan's elegant Carlyle Hotel and his father at a small estate he had purchased in Middletown, N.Y.

The sudden engagement of their son must have shocked them, too, but each parent received me graciously

Walking down a Manhattan street with Farley and his mom on our way to a restaurant, one of my heels got caught in a grate. As I tried to pull it out with some grace, the whole heel came off. Putting the heel in my pocketbook, I then proceeded to walk on my left toe as I tried to take normal steps with my right foot. Entering the restaurant to meet Farley's sister Liz I wanted badly to look nice and make a good impression, but there I was, hobbling along. Such an awkward start!

A conversation at the Middletown property revealed that Farley's parents were not the only ones who had something to learn about me. Sitting by the pool, his father asked Farley about the spelling of my last name. "Is O'Neill with one 'l' or two?" he asked. Farley had no idea, prompting laughter from his father and an answer from me. "O'Neill with two 'l's," I said, smiling.

Reflecting his acceptance, he kept referring to me as Farley's "bride."

With my sister being a nun, my mother had always looked forward to my wedding, and she had already planned for it to occur in our backyard. Now, that was never going to be.

Farley and I invited our families to the wedding in Korea,

but it was just too far for them. Nevertheless, in late September, my mother, joined by Farley's mother, flew to Washington to see us off. We were touched by their acceptance, love, and support.

With my older sister Marilyn

As a third grader

My parents in their late-50's

*My parents take to the dance floor at their
50th wedding anniversary*

Marilyn and me with mom at age 94

*With childhood friends (left to right), Emily Hurstak,Carol Bergin
and Margie Edson at Annual Memorial Scholarship Dinner
for Margie's husband Paul Sullivan*

BC School of Nursing '65 friends, (left to right) Betty, Ginny, Joan, me

Ginny and Tom McCabe, friends from B.C. and beyond

School nurse in Jamaica

Dr. Young Oon Kim

Father and Mother Moon

Ernest and Therese Stewart

Edwin and Marie Ang

A song from Father Moon at the 1969 Blessing of 13 couples

New York Unified Family circa 1968, (left to right), Carol Ann Debrotka, Maria Kiely, Diane Fernsler, me, Therese Stewart

8

Wedding for Peace

Love Your Enemy.
—Jesus of Nazareth

Japan

Our wedding was scheduled for October 21, 1970, in Seoul. When we left Washington, we headed not to Korea but to Japan, where Miss Kim had arranged a three-week, pre-wedding visit. She wanted us to see the activities of the Japanese church.

In addition to Miss Kim, we were a group of six American couples, two of whom were Japanese-American matches. Another couple traveled separately, bringing the total number of American couples to seven.

Exiting customs at Tokyo's Haneda Airport, Japanese members greeted us with warm smiles and bows from the waist. One Japanese brother approached Farley and me to say, "Furley Jonsa couple, please this way," and escorted us to an impressive-looking black town car. Our fellow travelers were taken to a humble van, causing me to feel self-conscious about our preferential treatment.

We would soon learn that vertical traditions abound in

Japan, so the treatment accorded us was the Japanese way of recognizing Farley's position as the American president.

Our hosts took us directly to their unpretentious headquarters in downtown Tokyo. Entering it, we were escorted through a narrow hallway to a large room where over eighty men and women of all ages were gathered, kneeling on the floor Japanese style, their backs erect, their bottoms on their heels, singing hymns. One of the Japanese leaders offered welcoming comments that were translated, and then it was our turn. Farley spoke first, but with my turn coming and my mind racing, I have no recollection of anything he said.

Somewhere, I had picked up a few Japanese phrases, so when my turn came I showed off. I began with "Watakshiwa Betsy O'Neill des." (Hello, I am Betsy O'Neill.) Those few words elicited surprised smiles and appreciative nods from our Japanese hosts. Feeling a bit more secure, I then became magically eloquent.

We met later with Mr. Osami Kuboki, a stocky man in his early forties who was the president of the Japanese church. With a warm personality and sense of humor, Kuboki-san had been the leader of a Buddhist sect before deciding to follow Reverend Moon. He happily shared with us the plans he had made for us to visit church centers and tourist attractions throughout Japan. We were going to be the beneficiaries of wonderful hospitality.

At early stops at centers in Nagoya and Osaka, we observed groups of young Japanese women and men, perhaps sixty or seventy persons per center, living together and devoting entire days to mission work. They had adopted simple, sacrificial, and purposeful lives. An unmistakable spirit of joy radiated from their bright faces.

We spent several days in a training center at the base of Mt. Fuji, where we did morning calisthenics, coordinated breathing exercises, and practiced a method for using our voices vigorously. We also hiked part way up the famous mountain.

Kyoto was a special stop, with its graceful bridges and waterways. There we participated in a tea ceremony with traditionally dressed Japanese women presiding over the ritual. It felt natural and beautiful in this appropriate setting!

We helped advertise a large anti-communist rally in Tokyo. Our role involved climbing on top of minivans parked in populous shopping areas and reading brief speeches calling for an end to atheistic communism.

No matter how short my talk was in English, the Japanese translation went on much longer. I ended my talks with a few actual Japanese words, saying loudly and passionately, "Sanka Shima Sho!" meaning, "Let's go!" to Budokan Hall, the ten-thousand seat venue of the rally.

Korea

After three weeks in Japan, we flew to Kimpo Airport in Seoul. From there, Korean church elders took us to a large training center on the outskirts of the city. With other couples from Western Europe, we resided in this simple structure until the October 21 Blessing ceremony. A different building housed the Korean and Japanese candidates for a matching ceremony Reverend Moon would be conducting with them.

Here we were introduced, some of us for the first time, to Korean cuisine, including kimchi. Not all Western stomachs were equal to the experience.

Between the time of our arrival and the Blessing, Reverend Moon visited us often. He certainly wanted to make a connection with the first followers from the West to visit Korea, and he also wanted to educate us. He spoke on various topics and especially about married life.

At one point he asked each sister to hand wash and dry the clothes and underwear of her spouse-to-be. This activity turned out to be the occasion for some mirth and bonding among the American and European sisters.

On another occasion, he invited us to walk with him to a near-by field. There he found a small grassy hill, which we climbed. We sat down together, with nothing being said. After about forty minutes, we stood up and silently retraced our steps back to our compound. The experience touched me. This was a person with a deep, meditative heart; I wanted to inherit that attitude.

In one talk, Reverend Moon spoke at length on the topic of loving your enemy. At the end, he connected the topic to our upcoming marriages: "Your enemy," he advised, "will be your mate." Huh? Farley and I were feeling happy together; I had no idea what he was talking about. I nevertheless decided to engrave the idea in my heart. I would be prepared to love my enemy, whoever it was, even my husband.

Our Preparations

As couples preparing for a group wedding in a foreign culture, we were destined to have many new experiences. One of them was uniformity of dress.

The husbands had brought with them standard Western garb: dark gray suits and red ties. The brides were to be outfitted once we arrived in Korea. Accordingly, one day a Korean seamstress appeared at the training center with a measuring tape around her neck and pins between her teeth. With few words, she got to work taking the measurements of each Western bride. With those, a white traditional Korean dress, a chimachoguri, could be made for each of us. She also took measurements for the white petticoats and bloomer undergarments we would wear.

Our feet were measured for traditional Korean rubber shoes, ones with toes pointing up, but with Korean women's feet being smaller than Western women's feet, such shoes were not going to fit most of our group. Problem solved: men's rubber shoes were ordered.

Before leaving the U.S., Farley and I had bought each other gold wedding rings, but the Korean church had already prepared gold rings inscribed with the church insignia on them. These were the rings we all were to exchange during the ceremony.

But how to obtain rings that would fit? One day Mrs. Moon visited us and addressed the issue. Pulling her own wedding ring from her finger and giving it to me, she directed me to use her ring as a guide. I was to put her ring on the ring finger of each American sister and estimate the fit. The imprecise process produced a need for two rings bigger than Mrs. Moon's, two the same size, and two smaller. I submitted my list, hoping for the best.

A few days later, the 14-carat gold rings arrived. Most fit, although two were a touch big. Not a bad result. Whew!

Japanese, Korean, West German, Dutch, Italian, Austrian, French, British, and American couples gathered to eat Korean food in a cafeteria at the training compound, and lines grew longer as more people arrived. Mealtimes felt like a meeting of the United Nations.

With the year being 1970, Reverend Moon had set a goal of Blessing 777 couples from ten countries in our wedding. Both goals would be reached, and then some. Ultimately, 791 couples came from all over the world to be blessed in a marriage dedicated to God and His larger purposes.

Prior to the Blessing ceremony, each of us had an opportunity to meet with Reverend Moon to confess any matters of regret or guilt. A day or two later, on the evening before the wedding, Farley and I participated with the other couples in a ceremony where we shared a cup of Holy Wine, representing our inheriting a new lineage centered on God. The ceremony took place in the early morning hours, and when it was over, I returned to my room filled with happiness. I lay down on my bed and closed my eyes.

As I was falling asleep, I had a strong spiritual sense of joy in and around me. The thought occurred to me that Farley's deceased grandfather, William Wallace Farley, and my deceased grandmother, Mary Doherty Laffey, were dancing together in the spirit world.

True or not, I sat straight up in bed and exclaimed out loud to whomever was listening, "Isn't it great!"

Blessing 1970

"Can you tell me why you are doing this?" The question was from a reporter for *Time* magazine, who was covering the story of the mass wedding in Seoul. He asked it while Farley and I were walking with the other couples in a pre-arranged order into the ten-thousand seat auditorium where our marriage Blessing was that day taking place.

Unable to stop to answer his question, I pointed to a sign hanging outside the entrance to the auditorium proclaiming, "World Peace Through Ideal Families." "That's the idea," I commented as the line proceeded forward.

I was happy to promote the meaning of this unusual event, and glad it might be noticed in the U.S.

Arriving inside, I observed an awesome scene: the auditorium, featuring a broad stage encircled with massive flower arrangements and multicolored floating streamers, was packed to the brim. There was a sixty-piece navy band and an organ playing Mendelson's wedding march over and over. The smell of fresh flowers permeated the atmosphere.

We received a warm reception from thousands of observers cheering and clapping as we passed. Koreans have a strong sense of family that extends to their entire nation, and as we walked through the auditorium, I felt the audience extending the status of family to us as their non-Korean guests.

I was grateful for the embrace of the crowd but experienced fleeting regret that I could not see my parents' faces among those gathered.

Once all the couples had entered, attendants brought flags of participating nations to the stage. Then Reverend and Mrs. Moon, again wearing long white robes with gold trim, ascended it.

Standing in front of us, Reverend Moon conducted a ceremony like the one I had observed eighteen months before in Washington, D.C. He asked us the same questions in Korean: Would we commit to lives of true love? "Neh!" ("Yes!" in Korean), guided us to exchange rings, pronounced us man and wife, and offered a heartfelt prayer.

The close of the ceremony included all the couples singing an ancient Korean folk song "Arirang," several congratulatory speeches, and three rousing cheers of "Monsei!" the Korean wish for ten thousand years of victory.

While the ceremony was on a grand scale, there was something very personal about it. Walking arm in arm with Farley as we entered the auditorium felt magical. I wanted to be with him for the rest of my life. Our exchange of rings was a moment of intimacy, perhaps intensified by the energy of thousands of witnesses. It was a massive event, but I experienced it with Farley inside our own personal bubble.

After the two-hour ceremony, we were given a bus tour around Seoul. On each couple's seat, we found a card and a small wedding cake. Each card contained a congratulatory wish and glued to the back, a leaf from a plant from Reverend and Mrs. Moon's 1960 wedding celebration. It was a simple yet precious gift, one offered from the hearts of the elder members of our Korean family.

That night, we returned to the wedding venue for an evening of entertainment featuring professional Korean singers and dancers. Less dramatically, groups of couples from participating countries sang native songs. Our American group, led by the musically talented Anne, sang several songs, including "Tonight," from *Westside Story* and "Getting to Know You," from *The King and I.* Our performances elicited an extended generous applause from our Korean hosts.

Round Shoulders

Several days after the Blessing, Reverend Moon invited the Western couples, eight European and seven American, to join him for a picnic in a mountainous area northwest of Seoul known as Cheong Pyeong, The Korean Church had purchased land overlooking a large lake, and Reverend Moon hoped to build an international training center there.

Arriving at one end of Cheong Pyeong Lake, we boarded a spacious barge which several Korean men rowed along a stretch of peaceful waters to the lake's far end. Reverend and Mrs. Moon preceded us in a small motorboat.

At our destination, basking in a warm October sun , we sat on blankets in a half-circle surrounding the Moons.

While we waited for barbequed chickens to finish roasting in a nearby fire pit, Reverend Moon took the opportunity to speak to each couple. Asking us, in turn, to stand up, he proceeded to give each couple some personal guidance.

When our turn came, he looked at us briefly and started to laugh. "Farley," he said, "you let your jaw drop and your mouth hang open. Betsy, when he does that, pat him on the lips." He simultaneously demonstrated the action himself and asked me to try it. Seeing me do it, people responded with ripples of laughter. We were all in fine spirits.

Turning his attention to me, Reverend Moon observed that my shoulders turned "inward." He told Farley to tap me on the middle of my back to help me straighten up my "round shoulders."

It was an astute observation. In the midst of this sacred, happy time, I was reminded of a difficult childhood experience.

The habitual posture that Reverend Moon observed was a result of inappropriate touching when I was about four years old. Although it took me years to understand why, I had grown up with a vague sense of shame. When my friends got their first bras with the intention of enhancing their curves, I got one that made me look flat. To the same end, I began turning my shoulders inward. I was trying to squelch my femininity by hiding it.

Now it was time to let go of painful emotions that had become embedded when I was too young to name them. I now had a wonderful life partner who made me feel attractive and comfortable with my femininity. God knew my whole life and my deepest needs. Yes, there had been an intrusion on my childhood, but I had nothing to be ashamed of and nothing to hide. On that day by the lake, I resolved to do my best to stand up straight.

The sharing with Reverend Moon went on at some length. When the food was finally ready, we enjoyed a zesty Korean dinner of rice, vegetables cooked with Korean spices, lots of kimchi, and well-seasoned chicken.

The food nourished my body, and the personal care shown by Reverend and Mrs. Moon for Farley and me, as well as all of their guests from the West, touched my soul. Returning by barge in the early evening glow on the lake, I felt a deep sense of gratitude that my life course had brought me to this point.

Returning to Seoul, we had a final talk by an elder member of the Korean church. "If you cause any trouble in your marriage," he warned us, "I'll come after you with a stick." "Wow!" I thought. "That's a challenge." Of course, I knew his words were symbolic, but they fired my determination to make my marriage work. Above all else, this would be my central life goal.

Back in the U.S., we learned the event in Korea had received no little publicity. *Time* magazine printed a picture of all 777 couples, with Farley and me barely visible in the front row. The *Washington Post* described a "Mass Wedding for Unity," and New York's *Daily News* captioned a large picture with the question "And Everybody Gets to Kiss All the Brides?" In Farley's home area of upstate New York, two local papers offered competing headlines: "Troy Native Wed in Rite in Seoul" read the *Troy Record*, while Albany's *Times Union* claimed, "Albany Man, Bride one of 790 Wedding Couples."

9

Public Life

On our return to the U.S., I went to New York and Farley to Washington. Complying with our church practice, we remained separated for forty days, following the example of Jesus who had spent forty days in the wilderness. After those days elapsed, I moved to D.C., aware that Farley and I would be living in a center with over thirty members of our spiritual community.

Our marriage was destined for an unusual beginning.

The First Night

Farley had chosen a room for us on the third floor of Upshur House, but his preparations had stopped there. He had given no thought to furniture, including a bed. "What will we sleep on?" I asked. With no clear preference from him, I found a two-inch foam mattress, suitably priced at fifteen dollars, hauled it home, and dragged it up three flights to our new residence.

This was not what I expected as preparation for our first night together, and I was starting to feel dismayed. When I asked Farley what time we should meet that night, it didn't help that he replied, "How about nine p.m.?" "Nine o'clock?"

I asked. "That seems so late." Well, not to him. Mission came first, he had much to do, and nine p.m. would work.

Even in this large center, I had hoped we would be able to slip away unobserved on this first night but that was not to be. Just as Farley and I started up the stairs from the community dining room, we encountered several members who knowingly wished us "Goodnight." I was embarrassed.

At that point, however, I knew we were their role models. We were young, but they were younger. They wanted to see in us what they hoped for in their own futures. Despite the awkwardness, I tried to accept their good wishes and feel grateful for their support.

In our room, Farley and I offered bows to each other and a prayer to God before we made love. The consummation of our marriage was the first moment in what has become a rich and blessed dimension of our life together. Farley was the first person I had given myself to, and our union as a couple filled my heart.

Returning to the community in the morning, happy greetings and knowing smiles welcomed us. We were not the only ones who were mindful of our first night together.

A few days later, we left for my parents' home in Waltham to attend the wedding reception they had planned for us. Over one hundred and fifty family and friends from Albany and Boston gathered in Framingham, MA in a large ballroom where we shared dinner together, cut the cake and danced to a small band. When we weren't dancing, I was happy to go table-to-table with Farley to connect with as many guests as possible. The memory of this happy event would remain during the next phase, a challenging one, of our lives.

Adjusting

My life in the Washington Center was quite different from what I expected or wanted. I had hoped for enough privacy for my marriage to develop in a way that deepened our love and reinforced our intimacy. With Farley as the president and me as his spouse, and with the two of us serving as the symbolic parents of the Unified Family in Washington and beyond, we were immediately called to a very public life.

It was not a life I readily accepted.

When we were alone, we were easily close and enjoyed our relationship, but I always wanted more: more time to eat by ourselves rather than with all the members, more time for a movie or a dinner out, more time to visit our families. Over the 1970 Christmas holidays, I was more than ready to visit my parents in Boston. Farley felt we should delay that visit and spend the time with the community to show our support.

I proposed to Farley that we move to our own apartment, separate from the center. The idea did not fly.

Our challenge was to reconcile the priorities of mission and family. Farley was mission oriented, and I was family and relationship oriented. This inevitably led to conflict that we tried to address without much skill. Our first year together was a year of tumult.

In this first year, we were in over our heads, but we kept swimming. We found a minister's wife who listened empathetically to us for twenty-five dollars an hour. I called some friends for a referral in the D.C. area and were lucky to find a well-known psychiatrist who had space for us. He ultimately guided us into a group where we gained more insight in resolving our tensions.

As Farley had no salary and no secretary, I tried to help

him by responding to letters, receiving phone calls, and counseling members. We had different ideas, though, and we often stepped on each other's toes. After nine months, we decided on a new approach. I would get a job and he would get a secretary.

Apart from our counseling effort and group work, it was the best decision we made that first year.

With my master's degree in psychiatric nursing, I was able to quickly get a job as a nursing instructor at St. Elizabeth's Psychiatric Center in southwest Washington. We now had needed income and health insurance to boot. That would prove important.

The summer after our wedding, we broke the public mold and took some private time, visiting my parents in Waltham and spending several days camping in New Hampshire's White Mountains. We hiked along paths dominated by magnificent evergreens and slid down cascades of water in mountain streams. With no one around, we even skinny-dipped in a quiet pool. That was fun!

In such special moments, I saw the potential of our relationship outside the pressure cooker we lived in.

At the conclusion of that trip, I felt I was ready to forge on against my grain. I decided that answering my call meant continuing to surrender myself to the reality of a public life. I felt God would guide me.

Farley too learned something: if he gave me a little more quality time, things would go better.

Seven-City Tour

On December 18, 1971, Reverend and Mrs. Moon returned to Washington, D.C. to begin their long-term mission in the

United States. Miss Kim, Farley and I, and others welcomed them at the airport with flowers and warm hearts.

The night after his arrival, Reverend Moon began speaking for seven consecutive nights to the Washington membership, pouring out his heart, sharing his God-given insights. He spoke on topics such as true love, Jesus' life, the progressive work of God in history and the ideal of a God-centered marriage. Soon thereafter he announced plans to do a seven-city tour throughout the United States, beginning in New York and ending in Berkeley, California. He wanted to call American Christians especially into a new dimension of their relationship with God and Christ.

Farley would be asked to travel with the Moon party, which would include Reverend Moon's translator, Mrs. Choi, and the president of the Korean Church, Reverend Young Whi Kim. Farley's role was to serve as the master of ceremonies, introducing Reverend Moon in each city.

Tea with Reverend Moon

One morning, several days before the beginning of the tour, Miss Kim asked me to bring tea to the Moons in their bedroom on the second floor of Upshur House. Arriving with a large pot of barley tea and several cups on a tray, I was welcomed in to find the Moons and their secretary, Mrs. Choi, sitting on the floor looking up at me with friendly smiles. "Betsy," Reverend Moon said, "Please sit down. Please have some tea."

I soon learned he had something on his mind. "I heard you and Farley have been fighting," he said with a kindly look. "What do you think the problem is?" Feeling the question reflected a genuine concern, my intuitive sense was to look first at myself rather than to any failings of Farley's. "Well," I responded, "I guess I want him to be more like me." Reverend

Moon laughed and then offered some guidance. "Your personality is only fifty percent. Farley's is the other half. You need to make space for both."

Pointing out that Farley had a strong chin, he continued: "Be careful. Women may leave when their husbands are angry, but they will often return. However, if a man leaves when his wife is angry, he may not come back." He then asked, "What kind of house do you want to live in when you get to the spiritual realm? Do you want a beautiful house in a valley surrounded by mountains with sunsets shining through the trees?" I nodded "Yes." "On earth then," he continued, "you need to live a life for the sake of others. Develop your deep heart, a heart to give. If you do that, in the next world you will have a beautiful home and a beautiful life."

His words touched me, and something in me shifted. Making psychic space for who Farley was, I recognized the value of his quiet personality, his depth, and his commitment to the Unified Family mission. I also heard in Reverend Moon's comments a gentle invitation to sacrifice some of our family time for the sake of a higher purpose; to let go of some private desires in favor of our public mission.

I left the room with a grateful heart for the path of my life and for the person with whom I was walking this path. I decided to find Farley and apologize to him.

I climbed up to the third floor where I found Farley in a deep sleep on our foam mat. Standing over him with tears streaming down my face, I asked for forgiveness for my part in our difficulties. My tears landed on him, but he remained asleep. Still, I felt I was sharing my deepest heart with him.

Even though I had an urgent desire to speak with him, I didn't wake him. I left the room, deciding to come back after he woke up.

Perhaps an hour later, we met downstairs, and I asked if we

could go to our room. There I told him of my experience with the Moons and of my changed heart.

In retrospect, I think that God had been an unseen guest at our tea and had spoken to me during it. I was newly appreciative of Farley and deeply appreciative of this Korean man who, with a loving spirit, had cleared away some cobwebs and lifted my vision.

Reverend Moon's first public talks in his seven-city speaking tour were given in early February at New York's Alice Tully Hall in the Lincoln Center. A large team of young, committed members accompanied him to New York, spending days, in bitter cold weather, inviting Big Apple residents to a series of three speeches. Happily, the hall was moderately full on each of the three nights.

Moderate attendance was typical for all the cities, except for the last. In Berkeley, a hotspot for social and spiritual change, more than eight hundred people turned out in the Claremont Hotel ballroom to hear Reverend Moon's message.

Numbers, however, were not the most important matter. The reality was that this largely unknown man from a small, distant country had now begun to establish a presence in the United States. His global mission was underway. From that perspective, the tour was a triumph.

It may also be said that the tour was a success on another level, perhaps an even more important one. Up until the seven-city tour, most members of the Unified Family were active because of their belief in the Divine Principle and the positive visions it offered. Now, however, we had met and spent time with the founder and had found our hearts touched by his big heart. The encounter forged a bond, one which in the years to come would deepen.

After their return to the U.S. later that year, Reverend and Mrs. Moon would be called Father and Mother.

And the Unified Family would adopt the name of its Korean counterpart, the Unification Church.

10

Spiritual Mother

I had a chance to be a mother before I had children.

In March 1972, Father and Mother Moon left to continue their mission in Europe. They were then to return for a time to Korea and come back to the U.S.

Before leaving Washington, D.C., Father Moon met with the group of members who had supported him during his speaking tour, asking for forty volunteers who would become pioneer missionaries in states that did not already have a church center. Their mission would be to teach the Divine Principle to potential converts.

There was no shortage of volunteers.

Father Moon also organized two bus teams of about twenty members each. They were to travel throughout the country to assist both existing small centers and the new missionaries with their evangelical outreach.

A New Mission

He had one more idea for supporting the work in each state: itinerant workers to travel the nation, visit the new missionaries, and lend them encouragement, counsel, and love. IW's, as they were later called, would be women, spiritual mothers for the novice leaders.

Meeting with members in one of the large Upshur House conference rooms shortly before leaving, Father Moon explained his idea and began scanning the group seated in front of him. He came to focus on several women, including me. "Becky, Anne, Marie, Diane, Betsy. Are you willing to be IWs?"

Becoming an IW meant major disruption for all of us. We would be leaving our spouses, our homes and our friends. Marie and Diane would also be leaving small children. Yet, we were being asked to participate in a new level in the development of a cause in which we deeply believed. Many of the new state leaders were young and inexperienced; this mission offered a meaningful role.

Such was the moment, and such was the momentum generated by Father Moon's leadership that none of us hesitated. "Yes," was each one's response.

"What does an itinerary worker do?" I asked. "Is there a job description?" I knew my question reflected a Western way of looking at things. The founder laughed. "Help them," he said.

It was a simple, broad instruction. In months to come, I would appreciate its open-ended quality.

How would five itinerary workers cover all forty-eight continental states? And where would each one go?

In such matters, Father Moon often resorted to a type of lottery, and in this case we drew lots. I drew New England and the Middle Atlantic states. New England! My home region! I was thrilled at the serendipitous choice. Turning to Father Moon, I blurted out "That's where I'm from!" His smile suggested he was happy that I was happy. His system had worked.

Afterward, the reality set in that Farley and I would be separated; for how long, we didn't know. We talked about it, but there was no question. We were ready.

In the early spring, Farley brought me, with a small suitcase, to the Greyhound bus station in Washington. From there I headed to Burlington, Vermont, my first stop on a thirteen-state tour. I was to stay three days in each state, move to the next, and then circle back around.

On the Road

The mission in Burlington was being established by Ted, a man in his mid-thirties who had spent his entire life on the West Coast. Being a state leader was quite a challenge for him, both in terms of his East Coast location and his mission. He had found a small apartment, furnished it sparsely and, like his fellow pioneers, had been sure to hang a blackboard on the living room wall. That was an essential for the main task, teaching the Divine Principle.

Ted was dedicated but he was facing difficulties. He was successful in inviting guests to his Center, but he found that teaching was a challenge. When he stood in front of the blackboard, he sometimes "felt sleepy."

My heart went out to him, and I decided to try to relieve some pressure. The first day we spent time talking, cooking meals, and putting up a few curtains. The next day I suggested we try practice teaching together, doing a simple version of the first lecture. I thought that if he had a clearly supportive audience it would help. It did, and it didn't. Sitting on a small chair in front of him I tried to be alert. But by the end we both were yawning!

In time, Ted's teaching skills improved, especially in front of real audiences.

Each missionary presented a different reality. In Richmond, Virginia, Andy represented the other extreme. He was a passionate missionary whose red hair was often covered in chalk dust from all the writing and erasing he did on his blackboard. He talked to people every day, finding them on street corners, in parking lots, or in coffee shops. I would go with him, quietly supporting his courage in approaching people.

As the winter of 1973-74 approached, I discovered a deficiency in Andy's situation: his apartment had no heat. Young, spirited, and inexperienced, his solution was to hand his chilly guests a blanket while they listened to the lectures.

This being a solution not likely to win converts, I advised him to move to a heated apartment. He spent extra time fundraising to finance the upgrade.

At the time, Andy had not yet turned twenty.

Each pioneer had his or her own approach to the work, and I saw my task as understanding and supporting that approach, whatever it was. On one visit, I found Lorenzo in Jersey City, New Jersey, undertaking a special period of fasting and prayer. I joined him for part of his fast and in his subsequent witnessing. We lent each other strength.

As it happened, my college friend Ginny, now married to Tom, was also living in New Jersey. On one visit there I called her, told her my reason for being in her state, and asked if she and Tom had time to meet.

Ginny was busy but Tom was available. The following morning, we met for breakfast at a local Denny's where, after initial pleasantries, I sensed an underlying seriousness from Tom. I had told him I was staying with a young male missionary while I was in New Jersey. "Betsy," he soon asked with concern, "what about Farley?" I laughed. "I am a mentor." I responded. "A type of spiritual mother. Don't worry!"

The exchange was an example of one of many misconceptions generated by my new lifestyle. The reality was that sometimes I slept in the same room with one of the brothers, but in different sleeping bags. In another situation, a brother slept in the bathroom and I in the living room. In almost no center was there a bed. I lived an austere life, but one in which I found meaning.

When I stepped off the bus on a visit to Peter in Wilmington, Delaware, Peter proudly introduced me to Nan and David, both of whom had recently accepted the Divine Principle. Standing in the bus station parking lot, Peter trumpeted my arrival with the claim that I "could answer any question" they might have. I was not sure of that, but I was happy to meet this bright young couple.

Learning later of their own spiritual journeys, I felt that the life courses of both Nan and David had prepared them to understand and accept Father Moon's new revelation. I thought that the invisible hand of God had been guiding them.

As time went on, many such young people were found, not only in my region but throughout the country. The students were ready, and through Father Moon and his missionaries, the teacher had appeared.

Through the leadership of Father Moon, the hard work and sacrifice of the state missionaries, the bus team members, and the IW's, and through the mysterious action of God underlying it all, the Unification Church grew rapidly and began to take root.

Special News

After about six weeks of travel, my itinerary brought me back to the D.C. area. This was a chance to visit Farley, and I felt a strong pull to do so.

As I entered Upshur House, I bumped into a surprised Miss Kim: "I thought you were visiting centers." "Well," I said, "time for a break." She smiled warmly and welcomed me.

Shortly before I left, Farley and I had moved from the third floor to a slightly more spacious area on the second. Our new room had recently been furnished with a plush gold rug, a pullout couch, end tables, and lamps. This was thanks to Farley's mother who had downsized and sent her excess furniture from Albany. We still had to share a bathroom down the hall, but no matter; we now had a comfortable, cozy place to meet.

For the two days of my visit, worries about the state centers were like passing clouds.

As the time for my planned Sunday departure approached, I proposed to Farley that we put on some rock music and dance. He was game. We soon had our feet moving and our bodies spinning, pounding down some of the tuft of that gold carpet. It was a high moment. We had a love to dance about.

Later that day, I set off for New England, again on a Greyhound. After a few stops, I arrived in Providence, Rhode Island to meet the leader there, a competent and disciplined young woman named Margaret. I was relieved to realize there would not be much stress during this visit.

In the middle of my second night in Providence, I woke with a strange, grinding feeling in my stomach. "What is this?" I asked myself. "An ulcer?"

But the feeling had come on suddenly.

The following day, I called a local maternity clinic, got some information, and bought a self-testing pregnancy kit at a nearby drugstore. According to the instructions, I was to obtain a urine sample, refrigerate it overnight, and get a reading the next morning. That night, I carefully put the jar containing my sample in the back of the refrigerator, behind other items. If I was pregnant, I wanted to share it first with Farley.

Early the next morning, I popped out of bed and headed eagerly to the kitchen. I pulled a testing strip from its box, dipped it into the jar, pulled it out and sat there waiting for a reading.

Before too long, a color on the strip emerged, the desired color. I was pregnant!

I took a moment to grasp the depth of the reality that I was now to be a mother, that Farley and I were now to be parents.

Not many minutes elapsed before I called Farley, thrilled to share the news with him.

Soon thereafter, I arrived in Boston to participate in the celebration of a church holiday known as Children's Day. The day now held even more meaning.

On the next visit to Washington, I established care with a local obstetrician, a doctor with whom I was able to continue care for most of my pregnancy. I told him I did some traveling. Without the words to explain my reality, I shared nothing more. I suspect he thought of me as a typical suburban housewife.

Farley and I soon decided it was time for me to graduate from riding the Greyhound. He borrowed a little-used Oldsmobile sedan from his sister Liz for his use, and I continued my travels in our car, a Volkswagen Beetle. Over time, the Beetle offered me comfort, security, and back-seat storage for things like V8 juice, pregnancy vitamins, and maternity clothes. It began to feel like my own little home.

Most centers still offered only on-floor accommodations, but some state leaders understood my situation more than others and gave me whatever extra comforts they could. Sometimes this included pillows and a real mattress.

It was Father Moon's practice in those days to meet monthly with the state leaders, bus team leaders, and IW's. The meetings were held at a church training center known as Belvedere, located in the New York City suburb of Tarrytown.

As fifty or sixty leaders sat on the floor of the large living room at Belvedere's main house, Father Moon would sit in a chair or stand in the front of the room, hearing reports on how the newly-minted leaders were doing and providing encouragement and guidance. He conducted these gatherings with warmth, humor, and good cheer.

Toward the end of one such meeting in the late spring of 1973, he suddenly called my name. "Betsy, please stand up." Knowing I was pregnant and not too far from giving birth, he asked me to come to the front of the room. I slowly picked my way through the seated crowd and arrived at the front, wondering why I was being summoned. "This is for you," he said happily as I reached him, handing me what was clearly a check. More than surprised, I expressed my thanks and took the check without looking at it. Returning to my seat, accompanied by happy applause, I had a wonderful feeling of being cared for. I then looked at the check.

Five hundred dollars would be of great help in preparing for our soon-to-arrive baby.

But the money was not the main point. What touched me was his fatherly heart.

The Datsun

The preceding February, Farley had been assigned a new mission, relieving him from his role as president of the American Church. For him, it was a welcome change.

Ten evangelical bus teams were now traveling state to state, and he was leading one of them. His team was comprised of American, British, and European members. In one of Father Moon's lotteries, Farley had serendipitously drawn the mid-Atlantic region, a region of five states that overlapped with my thirteen.

In mid-June, during my eighth month of pregnancy, our itineraries intersected in Huntington, West Virginia; this was several days before the bus team was to travel to Richmond, Virginia. On the night of departure, the team's work done, I lay down with blankets and pillows in the rear bed of a small Datsun station wagon. With Farley at the wheel and another member riding shotgun, we made the six-hour journey to Richmond. Approaching my last month of pregnancy, this mode of travel was less than ideal, but I was glad to be with my husband. My only concern was that I might begin labor as I crossed the mountains rising between Huntington and Richmond.

11

Real Mother

Richmond

Because our family needs were beginning to push against mission needs, Farley and I now started to re-envision family as part of our mission.

This new dimension started for me with our arrival in Richmond. While the state leader there had signed a lease for a large house, the lease was not to start until several days. In the interim, Farley and I, with his team of nine members, crowded into a small apartment where everyone was sleeping on the floor. Men and women were separated only by sheets draped over a clothesline stretched across the room.

My travels had inured me to the absence of privacy and comfortable bedding, but I now wanted and needed a bed and a room for Farley and me to be by ourselves. "Just be patient." I told myself, "Things will get better."

The spacious house we moved to overlooked a quiet tree-lined street. There, Farley and I settled into a second-floor bedroom with a real bed and a small adjoining room for the baby. What a change! Such relief!

I found a new obstetrician, took Lamaze classes with

Farley, and bought some baby clothes.

As an expectant couple living in a mission-oriented community of single men and women, we needed time to adjust; fortunately, the baby gave us some time. He would not arrive until two weeks past my due date.

Shortly before our baby was born, Father and Mother Moon traveled seven hours from Tarrytown, N.Y. to visit us and the team. It was a brief visit, but one that allowed us to receive some encouragement, share some food, and have a picture taken. The picture, one I still have, shows me as very pregnant and smiling happily.

I'm glad the picture does not show my very swollen ankles, a condition Mother Moon commented on.

Matthew

On a Friday night in mid-July 1973, I began experiencing contractions. Early Saturday morning, Farley drove me to Richmond's Virginia Commonwealth University Hospital.

I was in varied types of labor for close to forty hours, and Farley was there the whole time. He slept on the foot of my bed Saturday night. Beginning Sunday morning, he watched intently as the differing intensity of my contractions was registered on a monitor.

At noon on Sunday, my obstetrician responded to Farley's question about my prolonged labor:

"If she doesn't have the baby soon, I will have it."

"What do you mean by 'soon'?" Farley asked.

"We will give her another two hours."

Two more hours? Of this? I was already exhausted. At that point, two hours felt like an eternity.

Remarkably, exactly at the two-hour mark, the urge to

push came upon me. The baby was descending!

Push I did, for the next hour. At three p.m. our beautiful baby was born.

Hearing Matthew Farley Jones announce his arrival with a loud, defiant cry and seeing his shimmering body being held up before me, I cried warm tears of joy.

When Farley heard the same cry and saw the same image, he started laughing and clapping, walking back and forth past the foot of my bed.

A nurse soon blanket-wrapped Matthew and put him in an adjacent incubator. Looking over at him, I said under my breath, "Such a beautiful face."

Don't all mothers feel that way?

Soon I had the joy of holding him, caressing him, and feeding him as he nursed at my breast.

I had become a real mother.

———

I could not wait to call my parents. We also called Farley's. Happy news all around.

I was rooming with another new mother with whom I shared my happiness. She had just given birth to her second child. "I'm twenty-five," she told me, "and I'm having my tubes tied." "I'm thirty," I replied, "and I'm just getting started."

Prior to the birth, Farley and I had read *How to Raise a Human Being*, by Dr. Lee Salk. The guidance in the book stressed feeding a baby on demand as opposed to adhering to a rigid schedule. Dr. Salk encouraged his readers not to be afraid of spoiling a baby in its first year.

Nursing on demand had its challenges, and I didn't get much sleep. I made a chart tracking the sequence of Matthew's feedings, including which breast and the number of minutes on each: left breast, fifteen minutes; right breast, fifteen minutes, with each number circled. Using this method, my OB/GYN told me, I could avoid sore and cracked nipples. Helped by various creams, the method worked.

We had few clothes for Mathew, but during this hot July, a diaper and open top worked fine. Happily, we had been gifted with a beautiful crib from my parents and a necessary changing table and dresser from Farley's parents.

Two weeks after Matthew's birth, my parents and Farley's mother visited us. For my father, who had never had a son, it was a special time. After babysitting Matthew when the rest of us went out for a meal, he said, "I have just spent some of the best moments of my life."

My mother, now a grandmother, was also thrilled. Nevertheless, she remained a mother. "Why do you keep nursing him?" she challenged me. "He is wearing you out. You can get more rest if you bottle feed him." "I love nursing him, Mom," I responded. "I'll get used to it." I was standing my ground. I too was a mother.

Changing Gears

As of Matthew's birth, I thought Farley and I were on a lifelong path of loving each other and our family while serving God in a church-related mission. This is the ideal Father Moon had taught us and modeled for us, and this is what I felt God had led me to do.

The path proved not to be that simple. Farley had left his three-year post as the leader of the American Church a wounded warrior, emerging from his experience with his faith shaken. Six months later, no healing or clarity had come. Feeling little inspiration to lead the team, he thought continuing in the role would be a disservice to team members. "They deserve better," he told me. "I think I may just leave."

If he just left, I thought, it was unlikely he would ever take up another mission.

I intervened. "Why don't you go talk to Father Moon?" I asked. "Tell him what's going on; tell him how you feel." Agreeing, Farley soon arranged to travel to New York. On his return, he reported telling the founder that he needed a "leave of absence," and that Father Moon had ultimately understood. The meeting had preserved a connection, however tenuous. I was grateful for that.

The next morning, we asked our nine team members to meet with us.

The Richmond Center had a spacious living room with a couch and several chairs of different shapes and sizes. Farley and I sat on the couch and the team members gathered expectantly around in a circle. Farley explained something of his difficulties and that he needed to give up his leadership role. He, Matthew, and I would move to an apartment nearby, and a new leader would be appointed soon.

Farley's comments were met with somber looks and silence. Finally, one young woman, Marty, spoke up: "Thank you Mr. and Mrs. Jones for sharing this with us. We understand." Given my typical sensitivity to others' opinions, Marty's response was welcome. I was grateful for her words and the apparent support of the team. With tears in my eyes, I thanked her.

Reconciling

Less than a week later, we moved to our own apartment on the second floor of a large house on a tree-lined Richmond street. We had physical, emotional, and psychic space for the first time in our married life. In this environment we could be together, enjoy Matthew, and begin to heal.

In this new normal, we were two caregivers who could

respond to Matthew's every need for attention, food, diapers, and baths. We could spend time with our son without a sense of mission-related conflict or guilt. Farley worked at H&R Block, and we received some additional financial support from his father.

Farley was suffering from a loss of idealism and faith, and I spent hours with him trying to support his working through his confusion and pain. I had no clear idea if we could ever return to the life we had envisioned, but I would love and support him no matter what.

At one point, Miss Kim visited us. Commenting that Farley had a "unique nature," she went on to say, "He cannot be put in a box. He needs room to grow in his own way." The insight was liberating. It helped me appreciate not just my husband's serious side but his needs for space and creativity.

I prayed for strength to digest it all and to be a bigger person than I was.

Even though Miss Kim had helped me see our situation in a wider perspective, I knew we were in an uncertain place. At least for the moment we were isolated and directionless, unable to live up to our own expectations and those of others.

After Miss Kim's visit, I had a series of uplifting dreams. In each one, I was visiting an apartment where Father and Mother Moon were living with their children, and I was warmly welcomed. I wasn't part of their family, but I had a distinct place there, and I had a profound feeling of belonging.

The dreams encouraged me greatly. We might be isolated now, but there was a positive future. From this place in our lives, I felt we would be able to make our own path. I just had to trust God. Moving to the next step would take time.

Apart from the dreams, another unexpected, tailor-made intervention occurred. One evening, we took Matthew to a nearby amusement park, with the standard Ferris wheel, roller coaster, and cotton candy vendors. There, we spotted a muscular male swinging a sledgehammer at the bottom of an apparatus that had a bell at the top. If the hammer was swung hard enough, a projectile bounced up a rail to clang the bell. Farley wanted to give it a shot. Each effort cost twenty-five cents; he kept dishing out the quarters.

I realized halfway through this exercise that for Farley it was cathartic. He was working out his anger, pain, and resentment. "Yay!" I thought. "This is a gift."

Not too many nights later, as we sat on our bed talking, Farley broke down in tears. Identifying painful moments as the president of our church, the tears themselves continued the catharsis. Identifying his feelings, he could begin to let them go.

I think the powerful physical action of ringing the bell had opened a door.

Serving in the role of president had clearly challenged Farley, but I felt proud of him for all the problems he had tackled and the solutions he and his headquarters team had created. As a young man he had held things together in the two years immediately before Father and Mother Moon began their public missions in the U.S. and in the first year thereafter. In this moment of healing, I felt grateful that we made it through together.

Within a few weeks, Father and Mother came to Richmond on a public speaking tour and we met with them in the Richmond center. Our leave of absence had allowed for necessary healing. With a renewed sense that our calling lay with the Unification movement, Farley offered to take up a mission once again.

Farley's father Stewart in his mid-60's & mother Louise in her mid 20's

Our mothers sending us off to Korea with love

*International Wedding of 777 Couples
for World Peace, October 21, 1970*

Farley and I on our wedding day

American 777 couples in Korea: front, left to right Neil and Becky Salonen, David and Takeko Hose, Rev. Ahn. Second row: Farley and I, Hugh and Nora Spurgin, George and Anne Edwards, Ron Pepper (Darlene missing), Jack and Gladys Korthuis also missing

*Cutting the cake at our wedding reception
in Framingham, Mass Dec., 1970*

Hugh and Nora Spurgin

*In the Washington Unified Family Center
with Anne and George Edwards (left) after our return from Korea*

David Hose, Farley, Dr. Bo Hi Pak with Father Moon in
San Francisco, part of his first American speaking tour

With Father and Mother Moon in Richmond,
just prior to Matthew's birth

With our five children, back row Matthew and Cara
front row Farley, Harvet and Bow

Camp Sunrise staff members

Farley, Bruce and campers climbed to the top
of Mount Greylock in the Berkshires

With my Japanese sister after
a Bridge of Peace Ceremony in Jerusalem, 2004

*Sharing laughter with Father Moon after my report
on one of Mother Moon's speaking tours*

*Speaking as Women's Federation Vice-President
on a twenty-one-state tour*

With Mother Moon in Mexico City

Speaking in Korean in support of Korean North-South reunification

*With Women's Federation members Evelyn and Fannie
with Drs. Colin and Jean (center) in Haiti*

*Candlelight ceremony with 700 Women's Federation members and
representative North Korean women in North Korea*

12

The Hardest Call

In early 1974, Farley and I arrived in Washington D.C. with eight-month-old Matthew, settling into a two-room suite on the second floor of a large townhouse on Woodley Place. The two rooms felt like a safe womb within which we could develop this phase of our family life.

Farley's new mission involved working in the publications department at the headquarters office building near DuPont Circle in downtown Washington.

We shared the house with a public relations team of young women whose mission was to visit members of Congress and introduce them to Father Moon's vision for a God-centered nation and world. They were a friendly, attractive group of Japanese and American members with whom we readily got along.

Breakfast and lunch were solo enterprises, but dinner was a communal, family style meal with everyone around a large table. Sitting in a highchair next to us with a large plastic sheet protecting the gold rug beneath him, Matthew was the center of attention. At Woodley Place, he learned to stand and to take his first steps, looking up and smiling as his parents and spiritual aunties cheered him on.

Cara

Even before Matthew was a year old, I was ready for another conception. Farley, always a gradualist, was less so.

Soon, however, he had a conversion experience, the result of our escaping the house one night to watch "The Sound of Music." The large, diverse Von Trapp family inspired him. "OK!" he exclaimed, as we exited the theater, "let's have more children."

Farley and I had no problem conceiving. Not long after seeing the movie, I suspected that something was underway and made an appointment with a local obstetrician. Yes, I was pregnant again. I was thrilled that Matthew would have a sibling.

This pregnancy was so different from my first! No solitary travels. No sleeping on the floor. Rather, I had time with Farley and Matthew in a stable residence. Idyllic.

With Matthew in a carriage and my growing baby inside, on many days I took a short walk to the nearby Smithsonian National Park Zoo. Housing over 2,000 animals on 163 acres less than a half mile from our townhouse, the zoo offered accessible, welcome entertainment. Matthew and I growled with the tigers and chirped with the birds. Monkeys swinging from tree to tree earned Matthew's awestruck looks and happy squeals. Our visits there provided a welcome alternative to Matthew's favorite indoor activity of banging pots and pans he routinely took out of the cupboards.

A few days before my due date, my mother arrived from Boston. By this time, we had moved to a home on D.C.'s Military Road, sharing it with four other church members. It was large enough to afford my mother her own room.

Early on a mid-March morning of 1975, with several hours of labor behind me, I left with Farley for Georgetown

University Hospital. Several hours later, I had welcome news from my obstetrician. Lifting up the beautiful baby I had just delivered, he proclaimed "You have a girl!"

My silent hope had been realized. I was the mother of both a son and a daughter. Cara Elizabeth was soon gently nursing in my arms.

In our church tradition, parents perform an offering ceremony when a baby is eight days old. The night before Cara's eighth day, Farley and I covered a small table in our room with a white cloth. Adding fruit and a white candle, we created an altar. The next morning, we dressed Cara in a simple white dress and offered deep bows to heaven as Farley held her. Then Farley prayed, dedicating Cara and our growing family to God.

Thinking that my mother might find this ceremony strange, we did it privately.

Beyond such sensitive moments, my mother's presence was invaluable. She cooked, cleaned, and babysat Matthew. Particularly thrilled to have a granddaughter, she loved holding Cara and talking to her. A contributor wherever she went, she also sewed buttons for our housemates and cooked for the household.

I did not know how brief my time would be with my precious daughter.

The Telephone Call

During my early church life, I had heard stories of the wives of elder couples in Korea and Japan who had left their families to do mission work. These women had been living sacrifices, inspired by the Moons' own sacrificial life and the vision of a transformed world. I had sometimes wondered if the early

American families would be asked to make a similar sacrifice.

I soon had my answer.

About a month after Cara's birth, I received a call from Becky, the wife of the current American Church president. She asked about Cara and told me that American women, including mothers, were being asked to take up broader missions, similar to our Korean and Japanese counterparts. She further explained that a training program for the Americans was being scheduled at a retreat center in Barrytown, a small hamlet in upstate New York. A nursery was to be established in the same locale to provide care for the children of those who accepted this mission.

I understood the rationale. In 1975 Father Moon was striving mightily to expand the foundation for the American church. This was a time, in our still small movement, when all hands were needed.

However, the request was not quite being made of me. "Since you have just had a baby," Becky said, "don't worry about this now. I just wanted to let you know."

I had been given an out. I was not being asked to separate from such a young infant.

But I knew I was part of a community of women who would follow this direction, and I further knew that if I did not join them then, I would likely never do so. Should I make this huge sacrifice?

I told Becky I would pray about my options.

I did not need to pray long. As I sat down and opened myself to God's presence, I was moved in my soul; I would join the effort.

I did not have to go, but I had a deep sense to go. Even at such a cost.

Sign

What would Farley think? This would be workable only if he were supportive. "I am sorry for you and the children," I told him. "My sense is that I should do this, but I will do it only if you can support me." He listened quietly and said he wanted to take a walk.

Returning later, his serious response correlated with my own feeling: "You should go now as your peers are going now."

I agreed. Knowing myself as I did, I knew I needed the support I would have by acting with my peers. Without that, I would not have the strength to go in the future.

I would respond to this request and trust in God's grace.

"Betsy are you crazy? Your children are too young!" These were my mother's sharp words when I called my parents to tell them our plans. I had dreaded making the call, but nevertheless was ready to push the limits: would they be willing to take care of our children while I was away? "At our age?" my mother asked. "No."

I well understood their reluctance, told them so, and went on to tell them of the church nursery that was being established. Our children and those of other missionaries would stay there.

This information did nothing to calm my parents. During an increasingly heated conversation, my mother finally blurted out "Well, your father and I will disown you." "Go ahead!" I replied. "Do it!"

On that note, I hung up.

Ten minutes later, I called them back. With apologies on both sides, we calmed the waters and discussed the future.

Since my parents couldn't take care of Matthew and Cara full time, I knew the best plan was to have them in the Barrytown nursery where they would be cared for by church members. They would be with other children whose families were doing what we were doing; there would be spiritual and emotional support for all the children and their parents.

That would prove to be true. And to this day, I have deep gratitude for each of the women who learned to love our children, and other children, as if they were her own.

In Washington, Cara's crib was right next to Farley's and my bed. Over the next few weeks, I often rested with her on our bed, aware that I would not have such moments for long. It was our time to bond.

My decision, our decision, had given me a divided heart. I was caring for Cara and Matthew each day and loving them, yet also feeling the pain of our imminent separation. Snuggling with them, sometimes with each one separately and sometimes all together, my resolve was to enjoy every moment we had.

In early May 1975, Farley and I packed up our two children and headed to Barrytown. Before arriving at the training center, we stopped to visit Farley's mother and brother in Albany, about an hour north of our destination.

There, a striking incident occurred.

Although Farley and I had made our decision, I still had much ambivalence. Shaky in my resolve, on the way to Albany I quietly asked God to help me to better understand. "Show me something," I prayed earnestly.

We were staying at Farley's brother Stewart's comfortable home in Loudonville, an Albany suburb. Perhaps the day after we arrived, Farley and I gathered with Farley's mother, his brother and Stewart's wife, Penny, around a large family pool in a beautifully landscaped backyard. Cara was next to me in a carriage and Matthew was playing quietly on the side of the pool. There was a feeling of family, well-being, and abundance all around.

At a moment when I had turned to pick up Cara, I suddenly heard a loud, frantic shout from Stewart. Looking up, I realized instantly that Matthew had fallen in the pool. He was floating below the surface in his white playsuit. As my heart began to throb, both Stewart and Farley raced to jump in. My thoughts raced. Can they get him in time? Is he still breathing? Please God, save him. I felt if he died, I would die.

Up Matthew came in Farley's arms, looking scared, screaming loudly, but still pink. I ran to take him from Farley and held him in my arms, overwhelmed with gratitude.

I had asked God for a sign, and this was it. Here we were, surrounded by family in a beautiful setting, and yet tragedy had almost struck. I felt then that my best choice was to go forward with our plan. I would carry this cross, willingly offering my children for a higher purpose, trusting God that they would be protected.

Before we left Albany, I took a solitary moment in the guest room where Farley and I were staying to make a promise to God: "When these children grow up, they will see two parents who love You and love each other, and who will be there for them for the rest of their lives."

I no longer hesitated to live out the course that lay before me.

13

Barrytown Training

Saying goodbye to Farley's family, we headed south to meet with other families, especially the mothers who had also accepted this mission.

The training center in Barrytown was originally St. Joseph's Normal Institute, a junior high school and novitiate founded to prepare teachers in the Christian Brothers Order. The property was situated on two hundred fifty acres overlooking the Hudson River.

In addition to a massive four-story granite and brick main structure that had been the school, the property held a large Victorian mansion, two barns with horses, two smaller residences, and a building located near the river on the western edge of the property called the Gatehouse. A short walk from the main building, this was where the nursery would be.

Our first stop was the main building. Parking in its circular driveway, I saw Becky, the wife of our church president, walking out to welcome us. A woman slightly older than I and possessed of a quiet, dignified presence, Becky was one of the mothers who was joining the training. I met her just outside our car, introduced her to Matthew and passed a sleeping Cara into her arms.

The significance of my action suddenly struck me. Here I

was, offering both Cara and Matthew, turning them over.

As we walked toward the main entrance, Becky explained the arrangements. I had assumed I could stay with Matthew and Cara and have Cara with me during the daily sessions of the four-month training. I now learned the standards of the workshop would not permit that. Rather, in the interest of preserving focus, mothers were to stay in the main building while the children stayed in the Gatehouse with staff. Mothers could visit their children during free time.

Absorbing this new information and shifting my expectations, I headed to the Gatehouse with Farley, Matthew, and Cara. There I would meet the women who in the months to come would stand in my shoes.

Nursery

We found the Gatehouse abuzz with activity, mainly fathers and mothers exploring the house, meeting with staff, and interacting with their children.

"Is there anything special that Matty needs or likes?" The question came from Joy, a bright young woman who was introduced to me as we stood in the Gatehouse living room. It was she who would be Matthew's new caretaker. "He loves playing with other kids," I replied, "and definitely animals."

Mary, who would care for Cara, also had a host of questions. "She loves being close to me," I told her, "and I think she will love being close to you." I would later see her carrying Cara on her chest in an infant bjorn.

That first day, I made one request of both women: that Matthew and Cara could be in the same room. I wanted my children kept together. They reassured me that this could be worked out.

We spent the rest of the day and the early evening with

the children. While I wrapped close arms around Cara, Farley and I watched Matthew begin playing with some of the fifteen other children. I was happy to know he would have companions during my absence.

Later that evening, the parents met together in the main building. The trainee group would include over two hundred men and women, including fourteen parents: twelve mothers and two fathers. In the days to come, our parents' group would share meals, tearful talks, and times of prayer. We were a comfort to each other.

The purpose of the training was to prepare participants for a new level of evangelism. We were to strive to embody the loving heart of God for suffering humanity and to live that out by leading others to the uplifting message of the Divine Principle.

The training was divided into three phases: study, including practicing teaching the Divine Principle, a fundraising experience, and a forty-day pioneer mission.

Study and Practice

Our workshop leader, Reverend Ken Sudo, was a Japanese man about ten years older and two inches shorter than I. He was a gifted spiritual teacher. With a warm heart, an engaging wit, and a big smile, he imparted much inspiration. In choosing him as our main lecturer, Reverend Moon had chosen well. We dutifully listened, discussed the content, took turns practicing teaching, and participated in prayer vigils.

One of my fellow trainees was a young single woman named Laurie, whose mother had joined our church in the earliest days of the American movement. In following what she understood to be God's call, and failing to convince her husband to join her, Doris had left her family, including Laurie.

Laurie's experience represented an early instance of a mother-daughter separation.

While sitting in the lecture hall about ten days after the training began, I looked on the floor by my chair and saw a small puddle of breast milk. It was mine, and seeing it brought me up short. "This milk is meant for Cara," I thought. "What am I doing *here?*"

In that moment I was brought face to face with the conflict and the sorrow that was ever present within my heart. The lecture continued, but I was no longer listening. "Should I just leave? Should I go feed Cara?"

Then I happened to turn around. Sitting immediately behind me to my left was Laurie.

How long had she been separated from her mother?

I didn't know but seeing her somehow prompted comforting words to arise from within: "You will leave your children for a time, but you will be reunited. You will care for them."

I looked around further and saw some of the other parents. They may have been paying better attention to Reverend Sudo's teaching than I was, but I was sure we all felt similarly. I gathered strength from seeing them. Holding onto the promise that I would be with my family again after a time of working for God's broader purposes, I resumed listening.

Fundraising

After weeks of lectures, study, reflection and prayer, it was time for phase two of our training. We heard testimonies from members who had had successful experiences with fundraising, and soon we piled into vans to undertake a four-day mission to see if we could follow their example. Since during our upcoming forty-days of pioneer witnessing we were going to have to support ourselves, we needed this skill.

The fundraising group I joined traveled to Cape Cod. Having spent many summers as a child on Cape Cod beaches, my association with it was fun, not work, and especially not fundraising!

In our case, fundraising meant selling products that we would carry with us door to door, shop to shop, parking lot to parking lot. My product was a stack of small, matted prints depicting beautiful scenes of nature.

Never having been much of a saleswoman, this activity was a real challenge. I did not like asking people for money, especially for something they probably neither needed nor wanted.

Nevertheless, I plugged away for four days, having a minimal degree of success. Starting back to Barrytown, we passed by a beach. A beach! "Could we stop here?" I piped up from a rear seat. "Sure," said our driver.

Soon we were walking on the sand and wading into the shallows; I went further. Feeling so grateful that this experience was behind me, I walked fully clothed into a welcome wave.

Pioneer Mission

The final part of our training was pioneer witnessing.

The plan was that each person would be dropped off in a nearby city with forty dollars as seed money. We would stay there for forty days, witnessing and teaching. If we needed money, we would fundraise.

Apart from our four-days of fundraising on Cape Cod, I had been only a short walk away from the Gatehouse where Matthew, Cara, and the other children were living. I had been with them part of each day, but now I would be leaving for my forty-day training. Feeling the depth of this sacrifice for both my children and me, I determined to make my effort count. "If I'm leaving my children for this work, I will do my absolute best."

I was dropped off in Fitchburg, Massachusetts, approximately three hours east of Barrytown. I brought with me materials I could use for witnessing, and items intended to buck up my courage. One item was a recording of a talk by Reverend Sudo entitled "Witnessing is Love." I listened to it often.

Witnessing usually involved meeting people one-on-one and initiating a conversation on a religious topic. We were also encouraged to give public speeches, standing on street corners to proclaim the Divine Principle. Summoning courage from an unrecognized depth, I undertook this practice. Almost every day, I would find a central intersection, choose a corner, and then start to speak. Taking a few deep breaths, I would raise my voice: "Good morning people of Fitchburg!" I would then share my message of a new revelation and the vision of God-centered families as a basis for world peace.

I prepared a slightly different message each day. A few people would stop, taking in this strange phenomenon. If an interested listener emerged, I would later meet him/her in a coffee shop or at the library. Sitting opposite my prospect with paper and pen, I would explain key concepts from the Divine Principle, drawing illustrative diagrams as I spoke.

Fitchburg was a small town inhabited by stable New Englanders not generally disposed, I found, to hearing a new spiritual teaching. Nevertheless, one couple invited me to their home for dinner, telling me they had been touched by my efforts and my message. Their generosity filled my heart, and I felt that God was close.

Still, my initial efforts bore no real fruit.

One evening, seeing a young couple walking down Fitchburg's main street, I summoned my dwindling courage. "Would you be interested in learning a new religious philosophy?" I asked. "Yes," the young man replied. "Yes?" I thought silently. "Really?" Nevertheless, I said out loud. "Great!" Giving them my address, I arranged for them to visit me the following night.

When I had first arrived in Fitchburg, I rented a tiny room containing a single bed and a chair. It was there that I welcomed this couple the following night. With them sitting on the bed and me facing them on the chair, I pulled out my notebook and pen and proceeded to give them the first lecture.

The young woman seemed particularly interested, returning with her boyfriend for several more lectures. At that point I asked them both: "Would you like to attend a weekend workshop? You can get the whole teaching in one sitting. I will go with you."

The couple looked at each other for a moment. "Let us think about it," the young woman said. "We will let you know."

A few days later I had their thrilling answer: "Yes."

I had invited this couple to a church-owned facility in southern New Hampshire. There, experienced lecturers offered in-depth workshops almost every weekend.

Before leaving for New Hampshire, the woman told me of a cousin who was planning to go to Africa as a missionary: "I think she would like to hear this."

I would later call the cousin, Kim. Neither my student nor her boyfriend ever joined, but Kim did.

In such a way, God works.

On one occasion, I met a man in a Walmart parking lot who rolled down his window when I signaled him that I would like to speak with him.

He had a nice car, and I learned he also owned his own home. His prosperity, I would later learn, was ill gotten; it was based on his work as a recruiter for a sex ring.

This man wanted to change the direction of his life and was receptive to my message. He went on to attend both a weekend and a forty-day workshop.

He never did join our movement. Nevertheless, I felt I had been an instrument of some change. About that, I was happy.

After forty days, I returned to Barrytown, rejoicing to see my children and feeling victorious in my striving. My results were not overwhelming, but I felt my sincere effort to love beyond my family had attracted more of God's spirit into my life. I had made our sacrifice count. This was a gift.

14

Itinerary Work

Saying Goodbye

"Matty, Mommy is leaving soon, but I will be back." These were the words I spoke to my almost two-year old son as I walked with him and six-month-old Cara on a trail along the Hudson River. "Joy and Mary will take care of you and Cara, and Daddy will visit when he can. Please remember I love you very much."

I said similar words to Cara as I picked her up from her stroller, held her, and said over and over, "Cara, I love you. Mommy will come back." Whether or not she could understand my words, I could, and I needed to say them. I hoped the feeling behind my words would reach her, stay with her, and comfort her.

Two weeks after I returned from Fitchburg, it was time to say goodbye.

Reverend Moon had once said to Farley and me that our life course would zigzag, with alternating periods of spiritual connection. I understood him to mean that, at different times, one of us would feel more aligned with the Divine Will than the other. "God will grab the edge of a handkerchief and pull," he said. "In love, the rest will follow along." Through the Barrytown training, God had pulled my heart. Farley had been the edge of the handkerchief before, but now it was my turn to step up.

However, this raised a concern for me: "Reverend Sudo, besides the children, I am worried about my husband. My being away will be difficult for him." "Send him letters about your experiences with God," he advised. "Tell him about your inspiring moments. He will be all right." I accepted his encouragement and let go of my fear.

On the Road Again

My mission was a reprise of my earlier travels, but at a much different level. Since the days when I had traveled to support individual missionaries, hundreds of members from Europe, Japan, and Korea had undertaken missions in the United States. The centers I visited would not be one-person operations.

With many more young people living in each center, I had more to do. New members had accepted the Divine Principle, but they were facing challenges. They often had difficulties in relationships, sometimes with their center leader; they had to manage sexual attractions; they had struggles with the daily schedule and overall in maintaining their new faith. As I visited each center, addressing these matters often fell to me, especially as at least some center leaders were still young themselves. As a relatively older member and a woman, I was a mother figure trying to help new members learn, grow and survive.

Japanese Sisters

At one point after he had begun his mission in the United States, Father Moon had asked fifty Japanese women from our 777 Blessing group to immigrate here and serve as spiritual mothers in each of the fifty states. He now encouraged us, the American itinerary workers, to become friends with our Japanese counterparts, to support them, and to learn something from them. "If you do this, you can inherit much from them," he told us.

For this tour, I had again been assigned an East Coast region, now five states from North Carolina to Florida.

From Barrytown I took a train to New York and then a bus to Raleigh, North Carolina. There I met with the center leader and the assigned Japanese sister. Trying to put my own concerns behind me and invest in the situation there, I asked about the members in residence, their activities, and their challenges.

Before long, my Japanese sister turned the tables and asked about my life. I eagerly pulled out pictures of my young family. As I shared the photographs of my precious children, my eyes filled with tears. I had wanted to present a more composed image, but there I was, crying.

I apologized and asked my Japanese sister about her life. "Well," she said, "my husband is in Japan, and we don't have children yet." She and I were the same age, had been married in the same Blessing in 1970 and no doubt had the same hopes and dreams. Yet she was working apart from her husband, and she had no children.

Who was I to complain?

Each of the Japanese sisters I would meet in my five states was about my age, but their life experiences were quite different. In the case of two sisters, their husbands had left the church; the other three had husbands who were still in Japan. None of the women yet had children.

Each of these women had offered themselves with unquestioning faith, devotion, and love. I saw that their standard of faith was much higher than mine. Yes, there was much I could learn.

If I drew inspiration from the spirit of the Japanese sisters, they drew practical help from me. "Betsy-san, would you talk with so and so? He is struggling." "Betsy-san, could you give the morning service while you are here?" "Betsy-san, could you drive me?"

In time, rather than feeling disempowered by my separation from my family, I started to feel a desire to help the younger members to grow spiritually, to strengthen their faith and to stay on this path. I came to hope each one would achieve a God-centered marriage and a loving family. Compelled by observing the sacrifice of the Japanese sisters to see that I had a much-blessed life, I dug my heels in and committed to doing what I could.

So yes, I will speak to so and so, and yes, I will give the morning service, and yes, I will drive you and yes, yes, what else can I do?

The Japanese sisters were only too happy to have the help of an American woman who could speak English and knew our culture. In offering this help to them and to the center leaders, I consistently experienced God's presence and His work through me. Whatever help I was able to give, it was not my doing.

Eventually, in caring for the younger members and in helping the Japanese sisters, I was put in the position to offer a mother's heart. God led me to share the heart I had toward my own children with a larger community.

Our family's time apart took on deeper meaning.

1976

Early in the Bi-centennial year of 1976, Father Moon announced an audacious plan. He wanted to sponsor a "God Bless America" rally in New York's Yankee Stadium, filling the refurbished stadium's fifty thousand seats.

In the Spring of that year, I received a call from the church headquarters in New York asking me to come and help prepare for this event.

On New York City streets, a massive campaign had gotten underway. Hundreds of young members, having been summoned from around the country, were plastering walls with posters, speaking to individuals, visiting door to door and contacting churches. Their purpose was to invite one and all to the June 1st rally, hopefully to have a full stadium. Day after day, hour after hour, these front-line workers poured their hearts out and pushed their physical limits.

I was not alone. All the IW's had been called back from their mission fields to support the mission.

June 1st would prove memorable. As the crowd began to gather outside the stadium, the weather worsened. And as the crowd began to fill the stadium, a powerful thunderstorm struck. Sheets of rain soaked the guests, strong gusting winds sent the on-field decorations skyward, many ducked for cover. Disaster loomed.

In response, one very wet member – I believe it was my Barrytown teacher Reverend Sudo – started singing "You Are My Sunshine," soon joined by many others. It was a 1976 version of a flash mob, lifting everyone's spirits.

Fortunately, in due time the winds subsided, and the sun broke through, just before Father Moon strode from the first-base side of the stadium to the stage, located at about second base. From there he delivered a passionate speech, calling the American nation to a God-centered way of life and the creation of a God-centered culture.

Of course, the storm reduced attendance and many members were disappointed. The next day, however, Father Moon met with the membership, proclaiming the event a success, comforting those who felt that fortune had not smiled on their efforts. I admired his care for his members' hearts.

Father Moon seemed to be inspired by the actual outcome: despite the weather, more than forty thousand guests had gathered for the rally.

He soon announced plans for another rally, this one to be held at the Washington Monument. It was scheduled for three months later, on September 18th. Washington was to be my next stop.

———

The Yankee Stadium rally was held in the midst of hot controversy boiling around Father Moon and his movement. His teachings and vision had attracted thousands of young idealists who were often uprooted from traditional education and career paths, separating them from their parents' hopes and dreams. The Moon movement was frequently portrayed in the media with in a distinctly negative light. Alarmed, some parents were initiating aggressive actions toward their children, including violent kidnappings and deprogrammings.

As a pre-rally activity, the church had invited parents of our young membership to a meeting in New York to address their concerns. Named "The National Parents' Conference," its purpose was to provide information about the teachings and ideals of the Unification Church in the hope that parents might come to feel more comfortable with their children's participation.

Held at the New Yorker Hotel on Eighth Avenue, the conference included speeches, meals, and a free night of lodging for the guests. Over five hundred parents attended, including my parents from Boston and Farley's mother from Albany.

The president of the American Church at that time had asked my friend and fellow-IW, Anne, to coordinate the conference. Standing on the stage of the Grand Ballroom of the New Yorker, she addressed what was probably the parents' central question: "Has my child been brainwashed?"

Anne raised the possibility of genuine religious conversion and encouraged the parents to take a long view: "If your child has sincerely embraced these teachings, he or she may be in this church for the long haul. If your child has joined for any other reason, he or she will probably leave after a time. In either case, stay close to them. If you respect their decision, whether they leave or stay, you will not lose them."

Church leaders from Korea and Japan also spoke. Afterward, my father commented that he was not impressed with the "smooth talking" of one of the Asian speakers. My mother was less direct, reporting that she had "met a lot of very nice people." Their discomfort with the church persisted, understandably.

———

Aspirations for the Washington Monument event were larger than those for Yankee Stadium, and members were to be brought in from around the country and the world to ensure its success.

The challenge of finding housing for all the arrivals fell to me. With a limited budget, I located several small facilities, each some distance from the other. Knowing that having members in different locations would greatly complicate our effort, I petitioned Bo Hi Pak, Father Moon's right-hand man, for more money. "Dr. Pak, with the budget I have," I said, "members will be scattered all over. That will not work."

He understood my point and acceded to my request. With more money in hand, we found what we needed, just in time for everyone's arrival: an unused, empty hotel. Members from Asia, Europe, and the U.S. would have adequate accommodations, and campaign efforts could be centrally coordinated.

Shortly before the rally, Farley's mission brought him to D.C. as well. With our abundant supply of hotel rooms, for the first time in months, we could stay together.

Our son Harvet would be born the following June.

The September 18 rally featured a long program of music, a further strong message from Father Moon on "God's Hope for America," spectacular fireworks, and good weather. It attracted a massive, appreciative crowd and was declared a success on all counts.

During both the Yankee Stadium and the Washington Monument rallies the enormous controversy swirling around Father Moon caused concern for his safety. Particularly for the Washington Monument event, held on the broad, open area near the Monument with the stage facing out from the Lincoln Monument, some felt that his very visible presence at the podium could render him a vulnerable target.

On the day of the rally, a bulletproof room had been built under the stage where Mother Moon and many of their thirteen children gathered before and after the speech. Dr. Pak had asked me to be with them there, helping in any way needed.

The speech was delivered without incident, and I got back to the room shortly before Mother Moon and the children. There we waited. Soon Father Moon walked through the door, smiling broadly. As his children ran toward him, I saw him shed his suit jacket, tie and shirt, revealing a bullet-proof vest. Getting that off and flinging it away, he embraced his children as they all pushed in close in a jumbled mix, saying over and over the Korean word for father, "Abonim! Abonim!" Under his children's loving assault, he struggled to maintain his balance.

A few moments later, his smiling eyes met mine, the eyes of a young woman awed to get a close-up view of what this man was risking and to witness this intimate moment of family love.

15

Parents and Children

Family Respite

About a mile north of Red Hook, near Barrytown, situated on a grassy lawn overlooking well-traveled Route 9, lies the Hearthstone Motel. Two days after the Washington Monument rally, Farley and I met in Barrytown, picked up Matthew and Cara from the Gatehouse nursery, and headed there. At eighteen dollars a night, the cost of our room was in those days a stretch for us, but it did not dissuade us from a two-night stay.

We got to the Hearthstone in the late afternoon. Giggling and laughing, our children began excitedly jumping up and down on one of the two queen beds. I was relieved to see the bond between them, and grateful to their caretakers, Mary and Joy, who had protected their young hearts in their parents' absence.

For two days, we walked, ate, hugged, laughed, and played. "The four of us together," I thought, "is the kingdom of heaven." The sweet image of our togetherness became a snapshot in my head, a vision I could access when I needed it.

The time to separate arrived too quickly. Farley would

begin attending the recently founded Unification Theological Seminary in Barrytown, and I would resume my mission as an IW for my region. There I would have a special assignment that would bring me one step further toward understanding the hearts of other parents in a way that would deepen my own.

Church Parents

After the well-attended National Parents' Conference in New York, local leaders continued the effort to reach out to parents of our members. Our hope was to eliminate misconceptions and diffuse the intense feelings some parents had about their child's decision to join our Unification movement. Even if they remained opposed, we wanted to provide a more accurate perception of who we were and the ideals that were motivating us.

To accomplish this, we coordinated smaller conferences for parents all over the United States. After our Hearthstone reunion, part of my job was to plan such a meeting in my region.

We were happy to welcome more than fifty parents to the church center in Raleigh, N.C. With a group of a smaller size, more connections could be made, more questions answered, and more substantial bonds formed. We could give them contacts for ongoing communications if they had further questions. Many parents appeared to leave the day-long meeting with their fears at least somewhat assuaged.

I was a young parent, but I was growing to understand the hearts of older parents, and I could empathize with their concerns. They wanted the best for their children, as I did for mine. My task was to help them consider that their children were on a positive long-term path and that the current sacrifice associated with this idealistic path could lead them to a good end.

I could see that our members benefitted when their parents better understood why they were living and working as they were. I relished helping both parents and members in this way.

Apple Cottage Oasis

I remained in my region with an ever-swelling belly until about six weeks before my due date. On a warm day in late April 1977, I hopped on a bus in North Carolina to head back to Barrytown.

The seminary property in Barrytown contained a two-bedroom furnished house known as "Apple Cottage." The seminary president had offered this space to Farley and me for this leg of our journey. With a knotty pine interior, a spacious living room, and a small but adequate eat-in kitchen, it was all we needed to bring our young family together.

In the spring weeks leading to the birth of our baby, Farley and I shared quality moments with each other and each child. After months apart, Farley and I, and Matthew and Cara, slept together, ate together, and played together. We took our children on trail walks, read to them, and tucked them into bed. We visited other families who lived on what was now the property of the Unification Theological Seminary. We were living a "normal" life.

One day I heard Matthew and Cara talking nicely outside the front door. I was happy they were getting along but at some point I noticed the conversation had stopped. Silence is not always a positive sign, so I looked outside to find Matthew with grass clippers in hand giving Cara a lopsided haircut.

Since coming to the cottage, I had been paying particular attention to Cara, holding her a lot, and trying to make up for the time we lost when she was an infant. After this incident, I knew I needed to give both children equal attention.

After cutting Cara's hair short all around, I repeatedly told Cara how cute she looked. I can still see her looking up at me and smiling.

Harvet

Although he lived two hours from Barrytown, Father Moon often visited to speak with students. On a day close to my due date, I walked by him and the seminary president as they were seated together in the faculty dining room. "When is your baby due?" he asked. "Two weeks," I replied. He promptly produced some supplemental funds. "Please prepare well!"

In fact, Farley and I had done just that. We had taken Lamaze classes, now for the third time. He was to be my labor coach, helping me with my breathing.

My due date fell in the middle of the Seminary's June exam period. Perhaps predictably, I went into labor the night before Farley's final exam for a course he was taking, one on the life of Jesus. He had arranged to study with his friend Tony to prepare for the exam.

Knowing nothing of my situation, Tony arrived at the Apple Cottage door in the early evening while Farley was helping me with my breathing in the bedroom. "You go study," I told him. "I will keep going here."

Huffing and puffing in the bedroom, I could overhear the academic discussions in the living room. I held on as long as I could but finally interrupted their study session. Rushing to Kingston Hospital with Farley at the wheel, and feeling pain at every turn in the road, I wondered if I had waited too long.

Our son, Harvet Andrew, was a beautiful, healthy boy born kicking and screaming not long after we arrived. Putting him on a nearby scale and observing Harvet's active flailing of his arms and legs, the doctor exclaimed to the nurse who was taking over "Hold onto that baby!"

Soon after, Farley headed back to the seminary for his nine-a.m. exam.

I was now the mother of three and still a full time itinerary worker. This precious family time would have a limited duration.

After a few more months of deep bonding and sweet memories with my expanding family, I joined the other IW's at another conference hosted by Father Moon at the Belvedere training center. Leaders from all departments were in attendance, each giving reports and receiving the founder's guidance.

As the meeting stretched on, I sat on the floor with the other IW's, wondering what direction would be given to us. After long stretches of itinerary work, would the IW's, mothers all, finally be relieved of our missions and be directed to settle down?

The answer came almost at the very end of the meeting. Standing in front of the room with dozens of followers seated around him, Father Moon turned his gaze toward us: "Itinerary workers, please continue."

That was it. That was all.

They were words I did not want to hear, words none of us wanted to hear.

Throughout my experience as an IW, I often reflected on an experience I had with Mother Moon shortly after her arrival in 1971 in the United States. I was still newly married and had no children. Now, she had called me aside to share a picture of four of her younger children who were still in Korea.

She had said only a few words, but more were not needed. I quickly grasped the dedication of the Moon couple to their mission and the sacrifice they were making.

I was now making a similar sacrifice. As an itinerary worker, and during the times I had with my own children, I had experienced a mother's heart. I was a woman, a missionary and a wife, but at the center of my being, I was a mother. Recalling that moment with Mother Moon always strengthened my resolve.

So, I would continue.

I returned to Barrytown and prepared to head back out, initially to Wilmington, Delaware. This time, however, I took Harvet with me. Weeks later, I returned him to the nursery, to be cared for by a sister named Chris in the same house with Matthew and Cara.

I would have taken him further on my travels, but a call from our foreign missions' office had summoned me to a new assignment.

Special Parents, Special Child

A situation arose in the fall of 1977 that took me beyond U.S. national boundaries and helped me, again, stretch the boundaries of my heart.

It began with a phone call from Mr. Yoshida.

In 1975, a large contingent of young men and women had left their native lands, mostly from Germany, Japan, and the U.S., to serve as missionaries around the globe. To support their efforts, a "World Mission Department" was established in a three-room suite in the church-owned New Yorker Hotel. Mr. Yoshida, a kind-hearted Japanese man a few years younger than I, was the head of the department.

During the phone call, Mr. Yoshida explained that one couple who had accepted an international mission in South America was dealing with a very stressful situation, and he thought I might be able to help. Would I come to his office so he could explain?

Sitting in his office on the sixth floor of the New Yorker, I learned that the couple had given birth to a baby girl who had been diagnosed with serious impairments. She would not have a normal life. The baby remained hospitalized, and the parents were in shock. They were not doing well and were not able to care for the baby.

Mr. Yoshida's office had arranged for another missionary couple to come to the country to stay with the baby. The emerging plan was for the parents to return to the U.S. to receive care here before assuming responsibility for their daughter later.

There had been few experiences in our young movement to help us recognize that our families were not exempt from the difficulties faced by families everywhere. We would all be tasked to find practical solutions. These young parents were pioneers on this path.

"Betsy," Mr. Yoshida asked, "could you assess the situation and if needed bring the family back to the U.S.?"

Well, here was an acute need. My credential as a nurse qualified me. I was committed to help our members. "Yes. I will go." I grabbed my passport, my New York State nursing license and some medicine given me by a church-member physician. I then boarded a plane.

I was met at the airport by the husband of the visiting couple. On the way to meet the baby's parents, he explained that they had both been strongly impacted by their baby's condition. With their baby in the hospital, they didn't want to leave the country, but the mother, especially, now needed the kind of medical care available in the U.S.

When we arrived at the house, I found the young mother in the solitary bedroom, sitting on the bed. She had no energy to stand, but she smiled when she saw me; we explained that I was a nurse who had come to help her and her husband.

From her weary expression and rambling conversation, I could see she was not in her normal state. At the very least she was exhausted, possibly by the delivery itself and certainly by the challenge of accepting her child's condition. She may also have been suffering from postpartum complications that were not well understood at the time.

Whatever the reasons, I saw that she was near collapse. Crossing the room to reach her, I took her hand: "I will stay with you. I understand your worry for your baby." She looked at me in silence. I asked, "Has it been hard for you to sleep?" She nodded.

Her husband arrived and promptly interrupted his colleague's introduction of me. "No need," he said earnestly. "I know Betsy." We had met briefly in the U.S. before he and his wife had married.

Later, the father invited me to speak with him privately in the next room. There we sat on two wooden chairs separated by a small table. The room contained little else.

"How do you see the situation here?" I asked. He spoke with urgency to tell me he was suspicious of the medical personnel involved in his child's care and even wondered if some other mother's sick baby had been surreptitiously exchanged for his healthy one.

I could see that both parents were stressed to the breaking point, having faced in a foreign country an unfathomable, bewildering development.

What could I say or do to offer them relief?

To lighten the conversation, I asked, "Do you have a picture of the baby?" He reached into his wallet and pulled out two slightly bent photos. I could see she was her father's daughter. "Oh!" I exclaimed. "She has beautiful eyes. And she clearly resembles you. Can you see that?" After a moment's silence, he smiled.

During the conversation, I explained I had come to support the needs of his wife and asked him to focus on that with me since they already had solid help in caring for the baby's needs. "Your wife is not well," I said. "We should get her back to the U.S."

I further explained that New York headquarters would arrange travel for the three of us. The couple who was there to care for their daughter would bring her to the United States as soon as her condition permitted her to travel. "Please trust me," I said.

To my surprise he seemed relieved. "OK," he said.

Two days later, we helped his wife into a taxi and headed for the airport. Outside the main terminal, we lifted her from the taxi into a wheelchair and approached the ticket counter. Her poor condition did not escape the notice of the attendant. "This woman cannot travel," he explained to me in heavily accented English. "She cannot walk. She is too sick to fly."

My heart sank. I knew we had to get on that plane.

Frantically searching for how to respond, I reached into my purse and took out my New York State nursing license. For the first time I noticed that it contained an impressive looking gold seal. "See this license?" I said to the attendant, calling his attention to the gold seal. "This certifies that I have special training for situations like this."

I also showed him medication I had been provided by the physician in New York. "I will administer this as needed. She will be alright."

The attendant consulted in Spanish with two co-workers before he finally said, "OK, she can board."

We used all our energy to get our charge out of her wheelchair and up the ramp. At her seat, I took her hand and said quietly, "Everything will be OK."

In the middle of the flight, she became anxious; I quickly gave her the medication I had brought with me. Within minutes she was able to relax.

Later in the flight, as she sat between her husband and me, she took my left hand and his right hand, put all three of our hands together and exclaimed, "Thank you Betsy!" We all smiled and kept squeezing. Tears filled my eyes.

I felt I had been closely guided since I left New York. She was not alone in feeling grateful.

At Kennedy Airport, we were met by our helpful church physician; he accompanied us to New York Hospital and helped the woman gain admission.

For the next several months, I offered support to this couple as they continued to recover their health. Ultimately, their daughter was able to come to New York and a special caregiver was found. In time all three became stronger and healthier; they were eventually able to move to Washington, D.C.

Thirteen years later, I visited the family, finding I could not keep my eyes off the young lady their daughter had become. She was small for her age and dealt with daily health challenges, but I saw twinkling eyes, a happy face, and an energetic spirit that transcended her limitations. When we were introduced, she said, "Betsy, I know about you. You helped us years ago. Thank you."

This beautiful young girl passed away a year after I met her. She had been a bright, brave angel. Her parents had nurtured a wonderful family of six, all blessed by the life of their eldest daughter, their oldest sister.

With Farley in Hawaii

Matthew and Yunhee with Jazmine, Lance, Isabell,
Brayden, Selina and Darrien

Cara and Don with Ellie

Harvet and Kori with Abbott, Micah and Leyson

Bow with nephew Lance, nieces Isabel and Selina, and dog Arrow

Farley with Bow in the Canadian Rockies

Uncle Farley with Ellie

With (left to right) Kori, Cara and Yunhee in Maine

My sister, Marilyn with Micah and Abbott

Cara and Farley O. ready for surfing

Farley and I with Farley O. Bow, and Cara, Don, Ellie and their dog, also named Bo

Christmas, circa 1984 with my parents, Aunt Marilyn and Grand Aunt Louise

California Family Reunion, 2019

16

Coming Home

It wasn't long before I was again visiting the young leaders in my region, offering them whatever support I could. All the while, a big part of my heart was with my three children, wondering what and how they were doing, and longing to be with them.

Periodically, I would visit Farley and the children at Barrytown, visits that offered both relief and pain. During these visits I would stay in a guest room in the main building. In what unbeknownst to me would be the last such visit, I had stayed in the room, largely by myself, for several days, feeling it was too painful to visit the children from whom I would have to again separate. Sometimes I did not even take meals.

Apparently, someone reported to the president of the Seminary, a Korean man named Sang Chul Kim, that I was not leaving my room. On a day when Father and Mother Moon were visiting, he decided to pay me a visit. Sitting in my room in the middle of one afternoon, I heard the steps and voices of President Kim and Father and Mother Moon approaching my room. As they stopped outside my door, I heard my name. I recognized they had come to offer me support, but I knew I could not then receive it.

What should I do? I did not want to open the door. I did not want them to see my sad face.

I laid down on the far side of one of the twin beds in the room.

The door was opened. My name was called. No response was given, no presence disclosed.

Lying there, I heard the door close, and footsteps recede.

I felt their concern for me and appreciated it. I later gathered my strength to visit the children, to see them being comfortable with other kids and to again take my leave.

Within weeks of this event, a call came for IW's to return to Tarrytown.

Another conference.

Three Children

Conferences with Father Moon were often inspirational, but for the last few I had an insistent question: at what point would the traveling missions end? At what point would we mothers be able to return to our children?

Toward the end of this January 1978 meeting, Father Moon suddenly said: "IW's who have three children, please raise your hands." When the three of us raised our hands, we received new instructions, offered with a warm smile: "Please return to your families. Be good wives to your husbands and loving mothers to your children."

Return to my children! Words that spoke to my deepest heart; words that had an impact I can still feel today. A door had just flung open and I could now walk freely through it.

Days later, the IW's were invited to East Garden, the spacious estate that housed Father and Mother Moon's large family and served as the operations center for their worldwide mission.

Guests were regularly invited there from around the country and the world for meetings, holiday celebrations, and birthdays. On this occasion, the Moons wanted to express their appreciation for our service by treating us to a beautiful lunch and sharing some reflections.

Father Moon said many things that day, most significantly linking us with the sacrifice of the earliest Korean and Japanese families. "God's work does not advance without sacrifice," he said. "It is the path humanity must walk."

I was touched by his words, and grateful for them. Our family had paid a price, but we were not alone. I was united in a holy work with people from all over the world whom I respected and loved.

Toward the end of our time at East Garden, the Moons presented each of us with a gold ring. Mrs. Moon then took us shopping, encouraging each of us to choose a winter coat. Offering input, she pointed out colors and styles that were becoming to each of us.

Through my IW work I was put in a place to understand the heart of God more deeply. I missed my children, God misses His. I had pain. God has pain. That is my belief.

Yet, I had been given a mission that had also put me in a place to be used by God. Visiting my states, meeting with the members, I had been at least a minor instrument of help, healing, and support to others as they walked their individual paths. I had walked a path of sacrifice, but I believe God had used it.

Gatehouse Lessons

I was to return to my family, but where?

The Gatehouse in Barrytown was a two-story stone building with a kitchen, ample living room and two smaller rooms on the first floor. On the second floor, there were four bedrooms and a large bathroom, with a tub and two enclosed stalls.

Father Moon suggested to my fellow IW Nora and me that we convert the building to a shared residence. That was fine with us!

Nora and I divided things up. We would live in separate sides of the house, the Spurgin side and the Jones side, two bedrooms each, with a shared bathroom. We would share the living space on the first floor. The arrangement was unusual, but at least it was home, a long-awaited home.

The children of both families were familiar with this house, as it had been their home while we were away. Among them, there was lots of kid power and creative activity. Images readily come to mind of the children making hula skirts with toilet paper and decorating their arms with strands of it, standing on each other's shoulders in door jambs to pose for pictures, and rigging a can of ready-to-spill paint above a doorway. When challenged as to who instigated such activities, children of each family would blame the other. "It was the Joneses," the Spurgin kids would say. "It was the Spurgins!" would come the countervailing cry.

It took the parents time to learn how to manage our togetherness. The children initially ate together and bathed at the same time. While they liked the constant togetherness, Nora and I decided we didn't, so we opted to divide and conquer: each night one mother would cook for the whole group, but the families would eat sequentially. The children of whomever cooked would eat first while the other children bathed. Then the scrubbed children would eat while the others cleaned up. After months of this routine, the children grew accustomed to being primarily within their own family group and they began to settle down.

The boundaries were permeable. Nora's children, Andrea and Chris, would typically stay up later than mine and get up earlier. On occasions I had early morning visits from the other side of the house. More than once I woke up looking at two Spurgin children with bright, twinkling eyes only inches from my face. "Good morning Mrs. Jones!" they exclaimed.

Hugh Spurgin was in a PhD program at Union Theological Seminary, and Farley was in a masters' program at the Unification Theological Seminary. Both programs were funded by the seminary at Barrytown.

Farley graduated in June 1978 with an immediate destiny: the graduates in his class were to travel to England for mission work. Several days after his graduation, I drove him to Kennedy Airport and saw him off. When he would return was unknown.

I stayed behind with our three children, and a fourth one who was on the way.

Living in the same house with another family is no simple task. That summer, Nora and I faced challenges requiring trust, openness, and sensitive communication. We passed most tests with flying colors.

That we shared a common faith in God helped us get through differences resulting, in part, from our different family cultures. Nora, the oldest of nine children from a Mennonite family and a person of many talents, was stable, creative, and focused. She could sew a coat and even upholster furniture while all the kids, including mine, were playing around her.

I could be very social outside the family circle, but as the youngest in a small Catholic family, I was used to quiet togetherness at home. I needed that even in the Gatehouse, perhaps especially in the Gatehouse.

In this regard, I received a big assist from Farley's father, "Papa Jones." On a visit to the Gatehouse not long after Farley left, he asked "What can I do to help?" I hesitated to respond, but in fact knew what I needed and asked for it: "If we had our own TV, the children and I could have our own family time upstairs." Within a few days he called to say he had something to drop off. Arriving at the humble Gatehouse in his black Cadillac, looking handsome in a charcoal gray suit, he carried a late-model Sony Trinitron up to the second floor and set it up. It was an unforgettably generous gesture. "Thank you, Papa Jones!" the children and I shouted to him as he left.

Having our own TV was great. With it, I settled into an evening schedule of retreating with the children to a living area on the second floor where we would first read stories and then share TV time.

Providing the TV was, in fact, my father-in-law's second big assist that summer. Before Farley left, we had discussed being able to talk to each other frequently. Having no way to pay for the costs of transatlantic calls ourselves, we turned to Papa Jones. He was more than willing to help, arranging for our phone calls to be charged to his office. We took full advantage of his kindness, speaking sometimes twice a day. I would call Farley and say, "Sorry this is a two-call day," and then process a situation I was dealing with.

I have no idea what Papa Jones' phone bills were that summer, but they couldn't have been small. Whatever they were, I never heard about it from him.

That summer I took the children to my parents' house in Waltham where they were showered with attention. My father set up a croquet set for them in our spacious backyard and engaged them in other activities. My mother gave her love freely to each one with questions, humorous comments, and delicious food. At some point we all visited my sister's house in Maine where the children could be at the ocean with me, their grandparents and Aunt Marilyn.

Bow

In the years since our time in Berkeley, Edwin had completed his Ph.D and was now serving as the Administrative Vice-President of the Seminary. That meant his wife Marie was also living on the seminary grounds.

I called her around nine a.m. on November 24 to say, "Marie, my contractions have started."

Well before that day, we had planned that when the time came, Marie would take me to nearby Northern Dutchess Community Hospital and serve as my labor coach. After my call, she quickly got to the Gatehouse, took me to the hospital, and stuck by my side throughout my labor, delivery, and beyond.

Bowney David Jones was the product of a birth method known by the name of its founder, LeBoyer. The method involved dimming lights at the time of birth and promptly placing the newborn in a basin of warm water, simulating amniotic fluid. With Farley still in England, I promised Bow, as the doctor placed him in my arms, that I would love him for both of us.

As we had done with Harvet, Farley and I had agreed that we would ask Father Moon to suggest a name for the baby.

Bow's name is a derivative of a Korean expression traditionally said at the birth of a baby. It means, "Look, a beautiful baby has been born!"

Yes, indeed, that is how I felt.

⸺

Good news arrived in mid-December, six months after Farley left. He had been asked to take a new mission in New York, and he would soon return to the U.S.

Shortly after Christmas, I picked him up at Kennedy airport; he was glowing; "too happy," he said, to be home sooner than expected.

Farley's return was the result of a decision by Father Moon to begin a new speaking tour, this time giving speeches in English. This required that the talks be prepared well ahead of time. Farley had been an English Literature major at Princeton, so such a task would draw on his strengths. After spending some time at home with us in Barrytown, he moved to New York to begin this work.

⸺

Soon, another small family, a mother and infant girl, was assigned to squeeze in with us in the Gatehouse. Not long after, I had a dream about constructing more walls inside the building.

Fortunately, providence intervened. Becky, the church president's wife, was planning a small school in Tarrytown, much closer to New York City. "Could you move here to serve as the school nurse? There will be an apartment for you."

Could I move? An Apartment? Private space for our family? My own kitchen? Much closer to Farley?

Oh, yes! I could.

Tarrytown

With our four kids ranging in age from four months to six years, we moved to Tarrytown in mid-1979. Our spacious apartment, located on the third floor of a large manor house known as Gracemere, had two bedrooms, a living room, a small dining area and, most importantly, our own kitchen. The rooms all connected in a circle; on rainy days our younger children could ride their tricycles 'round and 'round through it.

There was no elevator, but this apartment was ours alone. So welcome. Yet, with several other couples with young children residing in the building, I also had a built-in community. A blessed combination of privacy and community.

With everyone contributing we were able to collaborate in creating an after-school program for the older children and a Sunday school for everyone.

For various reasons, our Sunday school was as far as we got with the school plan.

Of course, challenges would appear, mainly revolving around two factors: the absence of Farley and the shortage of money.

Farley was only a fifty-minute train commute away, but he was expected to stay in the City almost full time. He was home on weekends and away during the week, writing and editing during the day and witnessing at night.

At the same time, his work was a mission, not a job; other than being given our apartment, there was no salary.

With the solution to our cash shortage falling to me, I took a part time job as a nursing supervisor at New York Hospital, Westchester Division. The job paid well but undertaking that work while also being responsible for four children produced far too much stress. I was able to do it only because of the invaluable assistance of my third-floor neighbor and friend, Linna. Linna worked in a nearby church nursery, could bring Harvet and Bow there during weekdays and oversee Matthew and Cara after they got back from school.

Mrs. Mal Sook Lee and Phyllis Kim ran the church nursery school at Jacob House. They wanted to help us out as well and never charged us for the care of Harvet and Bow. Mrs. Lee asked only that I stop by her home in the afternoon to help her three teenagers with homework and help one or two mornings with infant care.

The seven hundred dollars that I earned each month took care of groceries, gas, miscellaneous and some compensation for Linna, a godsend who treated our children like her own.

As 1981 began, our fifth child was on the way. During my pregnancy, I developed gestational diabetes; my resulting large size made the steps to our third-floor location ever more daunting. Especially true with four children, their apparel and the groceries required for our growing group. I was feeling Farley's absence acutely.

It was becoming clear to both Farley and me that our situation was unworkable, and not just in this moment. We needed a long-term solution that would allow Farley to be a more present husband and father and that would also offer the promise of financial adequacy.

17

A Home of Our Own

Farley had come from a lineage of lawyers, including his two grandfathers, his father and his older brother Stewart. Prior to joining the Unified Family in 1967, Farley had completed one year of law school in Albany, New York. In 1980, he applied for re-admission to Albany Law School and was accepted. In January 1981, he moved to Albany, initially living for six months with Stewart and his family. Pending our joining him in Albany, he returned to Tarrytown on weekends to be with us.

Farley O'Neill

On July 29, 1981, our fifth child, a healthy Farley O'Neill Jones, was born at Phelps Memorial Hospital in Tarrytown. Arriving home with him, his siblings could not wait to embrace their baby brother.

Years before, I had seen the framed photograph of a family with five children set on a mantle in a welcoming home that was my safe harbor. At the time, the thought that I would also have five children had arisen.

With Farley O'Neill's blessed birth, my premonition was realized.

On a sunny day perhaps two weeks later, my sister Marilyn, now a former nun, arrived at our apartment with two good friends to help us get ready to move to Albany. With so much else to take care of, I felt like angels had arrived.

Within days after Marilyn's visit, we left Tarrytown. For the first time ever, including the births of five children, we would be living outside of church housing and in our own house.

Though we were leaving the church nest, we were not leaving the church. In the years to come we would work as a team, with both of us coming to serve in an unexpected variety of roles. Farley would become a long-serving member of the national church Board, would serve for a period as the New York State leader and the first president of the Family Federation for World Peace. He also served for many years as Chair of the Board of Trustees of the Unification Theological Seminary.

As I describe below, many missions would also come my way. But for now, we would establish our home.

Prior to leaving Tarrytown we had a dedication ceremony for young Farley. Many elders and friends, for whom I cooked breakfast, came to say goodbye and to offer gifts in honor of Farley's birth. Many just wanted to hold and hug him. The feeling of being loved and supported by this community was something I knew I would miss going forward.

I also knew that with all seven of us being together we would have our own wonderful moments. For now, it was time to plant our family in a stable place.

Settling In

We moved to the Albany suburb of North Greenbush. Matthew was eight, Cara six, Harvet four, Bow three, and baby Farley, later sometimes called "Farley O.," fourteen days old. We took up residence in a small Cape Cod style house which Farley's father generously helped us acquire.

One of our first acts was to bless the house and offer a prayer of heartfelt thanks.

Having our own place to live, seeing our children playing outside, simply being together. How great!

My parents visited from Waltham, jumping right in to provide us with needed items. Tables and chair sets for both the kitchen and dining areas appeared, thanks to them. Material blessings were falling from the sky!

With our own resources, we purchased a backyard gym set. Seeing the four older children climbing and swinging on it brought me great joy. They quickly claimed their new surroundings, riding their bikes in the driveway outdoors and playing freely inside.

Having arrived in August, getting the kids enrolled in a school was a priority. We visited several schools, both public and Catholic. In the basement of Sacred Heart School in Farley's hometown of Troy, I saw plaques expressing gratitude and wishing "eternal blessing" for several prior donors.

My eye stopped on one name, that of Mrs. Louise Farley Jones. Farley and his older brother Stewart had attended grammar school at Sacred Heart, and their mother had been a benefactor.

Our children had already participated in Sunday school in Tarrytown, receiving the beginnings of religious education. Since we wanted to nurture in them an understanding of God, seeing that plaque helped me decide that Sacred Heart was the right place for our children. Farley agreed.

Prior to Matthew and Cara's first day, I visited the school principal, explaining something about our different faith to her. She was very reassuring, explaining that several children from other faiths were already enrolled in the school.

I got Harvet and Bow settled in a half-day nursery school in Troy; later they also would later attend Sacred Heart.

The kitchen in our home was small, but there was space for a table, and seven of us squeezed in every night. It was bordered by a half wall and family room furnished with a couch and loveseat.

We lived in that house for eight years, a time when the family room couches proved their worth. Filled nightly with all five kids gathered to watch TV, eventually joined by a beloved black cocker spaniel named Star, the couches absorbed spilt food and drink, toddler accidents during potty training, dog hair, and more. Years later, when I decided to sell them, I found that even after much cleaning and deodorizing, they were hard to even give away.

Wanting to maintain our spiritual connections, we often drove to Barrytown where our children could participate in a larger Sunday school program. At one point, we invited a traveling evangelical team to pile in overnight with us. We also briefly hosted members who needed counseling.

During the children's high school years, we were blessed to live in a more spacious house within a bike ride of Columbia High. By that time, the boys had a lacrosse net and practiced incessantly in our backyard. All four of them were elected co-captains of their lacrosse teams during their senior years. Cara ran track in her first year and thereafter played field hockey and lacrosse. All the kids did well academically; Cara graduated summa cum laude.

All too quickly, college years started to arrive. Big changes were on the horizon.

Rough Waters

When we lived in Tarrytown, I was leaving Matthew's school one day when the mother of his first friend approached me. She explained that her husband was a policeman who preferred that their children "not associate with blacks or Moonies;" her son could not be friends with Matthew anymore. "I'm sorry," she said. "I understand," I replied. "Don't worry."

Similarly, the principal of the Catholic school our children attended there commented that Matthew sometimes seemed to be tired. "Does he have to march in the evening?" she asked. "No," I quietly answered.

Moving upstate, we thought we could put such difficulties behind us.

Even in our new location, however, we made clear our ongoing affiliation with the controversial Unification Church movement. We freely shared our background with curious neighbors and others we met.

In 1984, Father Moon began a thirteen-month prison sentence, convicted on what many considered to be trumped-up tax evasion charges. The day he went to prison, Farley and I were filmed on the steps of our house for a local TV news broadcast. That night we were on the five o'clock news. "Well," I thought, "It's all out there now. What will happen next?"

A lot happened next.

Setting my hair with a curling iron, a beautician asked, "How long are you and your husband going to stay in this town?"

She seemed to purposely burn my right ear.

Someone at a local school suggested that I "take the five children and leave."

My sense was to be careful of my reactions and avoid confronting anyone. With the hairdresser, I simply finished getting my hair done and never went back. With offensive comments, I pretended not to hear what was said, smiled, and moved on.

When a threatening phone call came about one of our children, however, I felt I needed to withdraw him from his school.

While such experiences were upsetting by themselves, what was really difficult was that Farley couldn't grasp their reality. When I described what had been said or done, he could hardly believe what I was saying.

"Farley," I would insist, "These things are happening when you're not around, but they are happening."

We were dealing with differing perceptions and experiences, and our relationship was becoming very stressed. "Maybe you heard it wrong," he said. "No. Please trust me. The things I am telling you are real. I'm scared."

We were at painful loggerheads.

One night, feeling alone and angry after a particularly challenging conversation with Farley, I left the house, walked to a nearby area, and hid behind some bushes. When Farley circled in his car to look for me, I remained hidden. I was not ready to go home.

Eventually I returned, but I still wanted to be by myself.

Even with Farley, I felt the need to contain some parts of my pain and anxiety. This was Farley's hometown. He had just completed thirteen years of full-time, essentially non-compensated mission work and was now making a financial foundation for our family. I did not want to rock that boat.

But I needed support, and I decided to get some.

I began traveling by train to New York to see a psychologist

I knew and trusted. I saw him about once a week for several months, an effort that proved helpful. My therapist helped me feel my anger and face childhood wounds that were magnifying my response to the actions and words of others. He also helped me take responsibility for any contributions I was making to my difficulties.

He offered me helpful affirmation and wisdom. "If someone sees a person like you as a threat," he advised, "your best revenge is compassion."

Reflecting on these words, I concluded God had given me a chance to learn the importance of "loving my enemy" in a real time. I would have compassion toward those who did not understand me and those who were not kind. That decision strengthened my spirit, and the practice allowed me to gain a clearer perspective.

Even though Farley and I continued to have different perceptions, we worked on overcoming the forces that were driving us apart. Farley came to understand how scary my experiences were for me, and that helped greatly. "Even if others don't want you here," he said at one point, "I want you here, and I want you wherever we go."

In time, our painful antagonism subsided, and we progressed. A Marriage Encounter weekend program sponsored by the Catholic Church was particularly deep and helpful. In an atmosphere where unknown couples had taken responsibility to pray for those in the workshop, we felt special spiritual support allowing us to openly face our different positions. It helped us get a start at being on the same team again.

18

Healing Steps

Goldie Lynn Go

"I think," I said to Farley, "that I would like to get a horse." I knew he was allergic to horses, but I wanted to learn to ride and to have the children learn. "You've been talking about it for years," he said. "Go for it."

I was working part time as a psychiatric nurse supervisor at Four Winds Hospital in Saratoga, New York, so I knew I could help cover the expense. I was forty- eight years old and moving on after five pregnancies. It was time to try activities I might like; and just maybe the experience would help me overcome some of my fears of living in the area.

As a child, I had often visited my cousins' farm in Wayland, Massachusetts. There they had horses they were happy to share with my sister and me, and there I developed a love for riding. In wanting a horse now, I was drawing on that memory. A horse would offer a chance for me to connect with my roots, introduce the children to riding and enjoy riding again myself.

I called my cousin Noel who had become an experienced dressage rider and teacher. "Noel," I asked, "how would I go about buying a horse?"

Noel didn't think twice. "Glory Be Farm," she replied, adding that it was near Portsmouth, New Hampshire. When I asked for her recommendation on the kind of horse I should get, she was equally unequivocal: "A quarter horse, a male quarter horse."

Farley and I traveled to Glory Be Farm, met the owner and explained our intent. The third horse she showed us was a female golden palomino with a confident gait. With a white star on her face and a light mane and tail, she was beautiful. The owner assured us that of the three horses we saw, "Goldie Lynn Go" was the most comfortable for new riders, because "she doesn't have an aggressive bone in her body."

I rode her briefly. She was obviously not a male, but I felt great on her, and Farley was fine with my choice.

At the time, we lived in a semirural area not far from a local horse farm. Several days after my first trip to New Hampshire, I returned with the owner of that farm and picked up Goldie, getting back around two a.m. the following morning. The owner took the lead to maneuver her into her stall. I suddenly realized I had much to learn.

———

Goldie served as a great teacher for my children and me. More importantly, she became a friend. Whenever I went to the barn, Goldie was there, eager to see me. If some people in the area did not make me feel welcome, Goldie always did.

I learned from another boarder at the farm how to groom and saddle her. I also learned to shovel out her stall and spread fresh hay. Overcoming fear, I learned to put a bit in her mouth.

This same co-boarder, a woman in the final stages of cancer, taught me and some of the children the leg signals for walking, trotting, cantering, and galloping.

My training took months, but each lesson, at the insistence of my teacher, cost only ten dollars. It was worth that and much more. With my skills developing, the feeling of flying around the riding circle on Goldie transported me to a place of freedom and joy.

Having experienced rejection early on in Farley's hometown area, I decided to speak of my personal history more cautiously and to seek to meet people on more conventional terms.

I realized that Goldie could help with this.

Our youngest son was then a first grader at Sacred Heart School in Troy. With the thought of offering his classmates a memorable experience, I approached the school principal: what about young Farley's entire class coming to the farm and taking rides on Goldie? The principal was game, as was Farley's teacher.

On a warm spring day, a group of about twenty-five excited kids, several teachers, and the principal arrived at the barn, eager to get started. I had rented a second horse for the occasion and, one by one, each of the kids was helped onto Goldie or the second horse. With big smiles and sparkling eyes, they then circled the ring.

After the field trip, we invited everyone to a barbeque at our home.

The experience was liberating. By welcoming others and sharing something of value with them, I felt I had moved from being an outsider to being a member of the community.

Goldie was golden in many ways.

Not Just a Diet

"Hi Betsy, how are you?" It was a childhood friend, calling from California.

Like me, she had struggled with weight issues for years, and our shared difficulty was a regular topic of conversation. Perhaps six months before this call, she had recommended a new approach, a diet whose magic I had yet to discover. "Not having much luck with the Zone Diet." I told her.

"No matter," she replied. "I found something different; it's called FA." She went on to say that with FA she had been successful in getting her weight down and keeping it off. She knew of an FA member in Albany, and she would get me her phone number. The idea of keeping it off sparked my interest.

Until my first pregnancy, I had never had a problem with weight. At fifty-seven years of age, however, having had five children in eight years and having faced stresses and worries related to mission work and family, I now had a persistent problem.

At the time of my friend's call, I was eighty pounds above my healthy weight. I rationalized the situation by telling myself that I had gained ten pounds with each pregnancy, ignoring the fact that my explanation did not address the additional thirty pounds.

Those last pounds might have been related to my children, but not to their births. The extra pounds reflected, among other things, the fact that I was trying so hard to control their lives—unsuccessfully.

In time, I sensed my body had developed a life of its own. It began to crave quantities of food as well as sugar products throughout the day. That was scary.

Over the years, I had tried all sorts of programs: Weight Watchers worked for my mother but not for me. A week-long visit to the Pritikin Center in Florida provided no long-lasting effect. Nutrisystem was another dead end as was a spell with Overeaters Anonymous. I also struck out with individual phone coaching.

Every doctor who treated me commented on my weight, noting that my cholesterol was rising and warning that I was a candidate for developing pre-diabetes. As a nurse, I knew that obesity put me at a higher risk for several types of cancer, heart events, and strokes.

Looking for a medical explanation for my excessive eating, I asked one doctor to order an extensive blood study. "There must be something wrong with me that explains why I am constantly hungry."

I was both disappointed and reassured when my blood studies proved to be normal. At least the worst possible outcomes were not at my doorstep.

Still, I knew I was in a danger zone, and I saw no exit door.

Then came the call from my friend.

"FA," I would learn, is short for "Food Addicts in Recovery." It is a twelve-step program that employs a spiritual approach to food addiction, especially to flour and sugar, and it emphasizes reliance on a higher power. Joining the program requires obtaining a sponsor and attending regular meetings.

I got my friend's information for the Albany contact and called her. "The nearest FA meeting is in Amherst, Massachusetts," she told me. "Would you like to go?" Not yet knowing her, I said I would drive myself.

The next week I arrived at a small church in Amherst, sat in the back of a group of perhaps twenty people, and listened as one person shared her story, showing pre-FA pictures of her very obese self. Her history was one I recognized.

She spoke of the FA solution: cutting out flour and sugar, weighing and measuring food on a food scale, and relying on her "Higher Power" for the strength to stick to the program. Indeed, she gave credit to that higher power for her daily victory over her cravings.

In years to come, I would make many similar presentations, showing pictures of my overweight-by-eighty-pounds body, and explaining how being in FA had given me what I needed.

I did not know my future as I sat that first night in the Amherst meeting, but I did know I felt that I had found a spiritual home in the group as far as food was concerned. As I looked at the speaker, I saw her eyes were clear, she was living in a right-sized body, and she seemed at peace. It all looked and sounded good.

Could this be an answer to my struggle?

Immediately after the meeting ended, I found the woman from Albany, who was also looking for me. "Would you be my sponsor?" I asked. She was willing. Standing in the front of the church near the altar, she explained the food plan, told me I would need to buy a food scale, and asked me to call her in the morning.

I was on my way.

I have now been following the FA principles for twenty years including, to be honest, a ten-year lapse. The program has given me not only a right-sized body; it has also provided an enriched spirituality in the form of greater trust in God, and in others.

I think if I had known what I know now when Cara was struggling with her marriage I would have responded much differently. Then I chose to live in fear and worry, now I would try to trust that she too has a Higher Power. Then I turned to food for comfort, now I would try to turn the situation over to God. Now, in this stage of life, I want to make amends to my children and to my husband for those difficult times.

A member in F.A. recently reminded me of a quote from T.S. Eliot about the latter years of one's life. Eliot writes: "We shall not cease from exploration, and the end of all our exploring will be to arrive where we started and know the place for the first time."

My take from this is that during much of our lives we are seeking to find parts of ourselves which have been buried beneath layers either of worry and fear or layers of too-lofty expectations. As we continue to explore in time and with faith, each of us can finally come to our true place, our true self.

FA has helped me immensely in this journey.

19

New Work

Having gotten through challenging times living apart as missionaries and now living together in our own home, our family developed a sound sense of a loving togetherness. This was my ideal, and my hope for all families.

The Unification Church had also achieved greater stability on the foundation of years of missionary work. There were now many couples and families as well as young single people, and the church needed ways to support our changing membership.

Camp Sunrise

"There is one rule everyone must follow," Sharon proclaimed as she stood in front of a group of fifty children on a grassy knoll on the seminary grounds. "You must have fun!"

It was the first day of summer camp in 1983, and Sharon was the new activities director. Several years before, my friends Marie, Linna, and Nora had begun a summer activities program for their children, numbering eight in all. Since then, other mothers joined in, and the numbers at the camp had grown. The program had acquired a name: Camp Sunrise.

The seminary property included a large soccer field, wooded

trails winding along the Hudson River, an outdoor swimming pool, a tennis court, horse stables, riding ring, an indoor basketball court, and spaces for arts and crafts. All this provided ample opportunities for the campers to honor Sharon's directive that they have fun.

In 1983, other responsibilities had asserted their claim on the original camp founders. "Betsy," Marie asked during a phone call the preceding spring, "would you and Farley be able to take on the camp?"

For me, there was no question.

By that year, with our oldest child turning ten and our youngest two, I felt free enough, and even eager, for a substantial project like this.

I also saw the summer camp as an opportunity to address the question of how to effectively pass on to my children something of the faith I had found to be so valuable.

Matthew had already participated in the camp for two summers, and after his second experience he reported a newfound pride in our church. If Matthew could have such an experience, others could too. I was happy to help the children of church families appreciate their spiritual heritage.

Also, in his first two years, Matthew had bonded closely with peers and had found role models in certain older boys. These were relationships I wanted for him and for other children, including my own.

Farley and I ran the camp together for two years. Since he was still lawyering full-time, I headed it up myself for another two years.

Resources to run Camp Sunrise were limited. Many church families were engaged in mission work, so finances were thin, and we needed to keep the camp fees small. We didn't pay the staff, many of whom were parents. Everyone, whether cooks, dish washers, group leaders, lifeguards, or sports instructors simply volunteered their service.

Fun was critical for the kids, and religious education was important to the parents. To this end, interactive classes were held each morning to introduce aspects of the Divine Principle. Underlying everything was the goal of helping the children understand and experience the reality of God.

We also worked at values formation. At the beginning of each year, a theme was announced. One year it was "Courage." Another it was "Builders of the Universe," based on a popular "Masters of the Universe" television series. That summer, the children were taught to build their spirits through developing healthy attitudes.

A highlight each year was the unveiling on the first night of a new T-shirt with a unique logo. I loved seeing their excitement as the campers – many from different nationalities and races – tried on shirts they would share in common. New campers especially could feel they belonged by donning their shirts. Much later, I learned a few campers had held onto several years' worth of T-shirts.

In the spring of my final year as camp director, I wrote a letter to the heads of several church-related businesses, explaining how important the camp was for the children and yet how restricted we were in what we could offer: "Would your business be willing to make a donation?" To my amazement we received over three thousand dollars by the beginning of camp.

In the 1980's, New Jersey's "Action Park" was the go-to destination for kids' fun. "Why not?" I thought. I called the Park, got a discount, paid for large buses to chauffeur us, and made a day of it. Heading out on the buses, the spirit was exuberant; after we arrived the joy was palpable as the kids ran from one attraction to the next. "Mrs. Jones," one boy exclaimed at day's end, "this was the best day of my life!"

Three thousand dollars was a small price to pay for a child to have a memory like that.

The camp provided other memorable moments. Each summer, the children would create skits reflecting some aspect of their lives. One summer, when two of the Moon children, Kwon Jin and Sun Jin attended, a skit had them playing the role of their parents and other campers the role of their children. In the skit, the parents, about to leave for a mission abroad, knelt in prayer for their children. Their children, learning their parents were leaving, hugged their parents as they said farewell. We knew this touching scene captured the reality of the Moon family, and many of our own families.

Matching

In those days, membership of the Unification Church more and more transitioned to include couples and families, not just single idealists. Although some already-married couples joined the movement, most families began with one of Reverend Moon's matching ceremonies. I had the chance to be involved in more than one.

"How tall are you?" Father Moon asked a young woman from Japan as she stood nervously perhaps ten feet away from him in a small group of other young women. As he asked the question, he was holding the arm of a six-foot, four-inch-tall American man, a young man for whom he was seeking an appropriate marriage partner. Would this Japanese lady be far too short?

Apparently not. With her answer given, Reverend Moon summoned her to where he stood and looked carefully at the potential couple together. Concluding they matched well, he waived them on to talk to each other about the possibility.

Now what other American brothers would like to be matched with a Japanese sister?

The scene was unfolding in the Grand Ballroom of the New Yorker Hotel, a room illumined by a series of crystal chandeliers dating back to the hotel's construction during the 1920's Jazz Age.

Now, over two thousand members from six continents sat quietly and prayerfully on that carpet, men on one side, women on the other, with a wide aisle in between. Each faithful member was waiting with great anticipation.

Walking up and down the aisle, looking intently to his left and then to his right, was Father Moon. Asking a young male member to stand, he would then turn to look among the young women to select a suitable match. On occasion he would ask small groups to stand: "All seminary graduates, male and female, please stand up," or "Anyone who would like an international match (or an interracial match) please stand up."

An interracial or international match? This was Father Moon's ideal. The world could be brought together, and peace could be brought closer, through such God-centered couples.

Blessed Families

The matching ceremony that day had begun hours earlier when the Moons arrived in the ballroom accompanied by several senior Korean and Japanese leaders. Welcomed with warm applause, Father Moon had immediately begun to speak on his favorite topics: true love and God-centered marriage.

From one angle or another, he taught on these topics incessantly. As I have mentioned, for him, realizing true love in marriage was the central purpose of God's creative undertaking. God's love was to be embodied in the marital, parental, and sibling relationships of a true family. The Spirit of God would take up residence on earth through such families.

On this bright morning, Father Moon spoke at length, and even though the moment was a serious one, he became comedic. His talk alternately had his listeners laughing out loud, thinking seriously, or feeling inspired. He taught that God was "color blind," that seeking the will of God would help couples "step into love," and that an ideal couple often started out with the "worst husband or wife." As partners worked together to help each other become ideal mates, God would give each one a "medal of honor in love."

At the conclusion of his talk, he offered a heartfelt, tearful prayer, asking the blessing of heaven for each person present and for the process about to take place.

As the only sacrament in the church, the marriage Blessing was believed to be a channel of divine grace. Receiving it was held in the highest regard by church members.

To participate in a matching, participants had to meet certain criteria. Each one must have dedicated three years to a church mission, remained sexually abstinent, and introduced three "spiritual children" to the Divine Principle. Also, each member was to have completed a seven-day fast and be at least twenty-two years old.

The purpose of all this was to ensure that marriage candidates had established at least some degree of a spiritual foundation as a basis for their marriage. The ideal was to nurture a vertical relationship with God before attempting to develop a horizontal relationship with a partner. God, not self, was to be at the center of marriage.

Based on such criteria, all those who now sat in the New Yorker Ballroom had qualified.

———

Upon being matched, each couple had the opportunity to retreat to an upstairs balcony where they could sit and talk. Translators and counselors were available as needed. I and several women from previous blessings were also there. The final decision to accept the match or not was up to each couple, but most accepted. Such was the trust they had in Reverend Moon's care for them and in his intuitive gifts.

The tall American at this matching ceremony later wrote a testimony about the process in a church magazine: "We bowed to Father. I did not even look at her. I only knew she was Japanese. We simply went up to the balcony to talk." Underlying his experience, he wrote that he had felt "so much love from Father."

With some breaks, the matching process went on through the entire day and into the night. By noon the next day, the New Yorker Hotel lobby was full of smiling couples starting to get to know one another. Some were alone, others in small groups; a few were referencing foreign language dictionaries, attempting to connect with a partner who spoke a different language.

For all of them, a new world was beginning.

A New Department

How could the church support the journey of these young couples?

In Korea and Japan, our church had developed an office

known as the Blessed Family Department. Following suit, in the late 1970's, members in the U.S. initially developed "Blessing Committees," and then set out to develop a more official national department.

One day in the mid-1980's, I received a phone call from the U.S. church headquarters. A Blessed Family Department, soon to be referred to as the BFD, was being established in New York, with my friend Nora as its initial director. "Would you be willing to be her assistant?" I was asked. I was living three hours north of New York, but the prospect attracted me. I would be happy to work with Nora again, especially in providing support to church individuals and couples. I readily accepted.

I devoted myself to the work of the BFD for nine years.

The BFD office served as a reference point for education, communication, and counseling. Nora held a master's degree in psychiatric social work, and I held a master's in psychiatric nursing, so we brought relevant backgrounds to the mission of guiding younger couples in their marital journeys.

I never thought we were alone in our efforts; my experience was that we were involved in a divine partnership with God. I found that Heaven was invested in the success of these couples; those of us assigned to work with them were simply available instruments of God's loving care.

Some couples struggled with problems all couples face. Others faced the additional challenge of an international, interracial, or intercultural marriage. These couples had sought to do something extra in bringing nations and races closer. It was our privilege to help them if we could.

Nora and I shared the counseling duties. On the days I was in

New York, I sometimes met with individuals and sometimes with couples. If there was a problem within a Japanese-American couple I would arrange for a Japanese counselor to join us.

Unification members were not perfect, and our office also became a place of confession, especially of sexual transgressions. Hearing about these problems was painful, but the fact that they were being disclosed meant healing could begin. Just as priests listened to confessions and gave penances, Nora and I guided couples to actions such as prayer and fasting. With repentance and forgiveness, couples could begin anew.

I saw my work in these instances as facilitating reconciliation between human beings and God. Sometimes I felt like I was carrying a large black plastic bag, saying, "Go ahead. Put it in here. God will take it away!"

I realized through this time that God was a loving, forgiving God, and I learned not to judge. Where sincere repentance and commitment were present, divine mercy could heal almost any situation.

Not every couple we saw succeeded, but most did.

As I gained experience in the BFD, I came to feel that my whole life, including my religious and psychiatric training, my experience as an itinerary worker, and my experience as a wife and mother, had all prepared me for this mission. Years before, I had sensed I would work for the family of man beyond the bounds of my nation and my Catholic faith. Working with couples, especially the international and interracial ones, fulfilled that sense. I cherished the work.

After several years, Nora moved to Philadelphia, and I inherited the multi-faceted role she had pioneered. During my time as the director of the BFD, I was blessed with the help of Alice, a gifted assistant who brought needed organizational skills to the office and much spiritual support to visitors. Her work left me free to offer counseling, prepare talks and workshops, and work on developing the BFD as an increasingly useful resource for church couples and families. Wanting to supplement my background in psychiatric nursing with more study on family dynamics, I began a course of study at the Ackerman Institute for Family Therapy in New York. This helped me understand more about how to help couples resolve conflicts. I shared the information I gained with two other women, Debby and Lynn, who had also volunteered to help couples.

In years to come Farley and I, Debby and Lynn, and many other individuals and couples would become certified in a variety of marriage enrichment programs. With our teachings placing supreme value on achieving true love in marriage and family, the BFD programs played a vital role in helping couples obtain the information and skills needed in working out their marriages.

20

Bridge of Peace

In the spring of 1992, Mother Moon founded a new organization to mobilize the energy of women in the cause of world peace. She called it the Women's Federation for World Peace, and asked Nora to serve as its first American president. She also asked two Korean, one Japanese, and two American women to serve as vice-presidents. I was one of the Americans she called on.

Mother Moon's conviction was that in the 21st century women would have a critical role in the cause of peace. Promoting this theme, she thereafter traveled throughout the U.S. and the world giving speeches on the topics of true love, family solidarity, and the role of women in nurturing world peace. On her first speaking tour Nora and I had the privilege to travel with her to many cities in the U.S, and with the goal that her speech would be given in all 50 states, some of us later traveled as her representatives to states she had been unable to visit.

The Women's Federation eventually achieved recognition by the United Nations as a Non-Governmental Organization, or NGO, entitled to participate in events the UN sponsored. One of its signature works would be the Bridge of Peace.

Sisterhood

Roughly two years after the founding of the Women's Federation, I received a call from a close associate of the Moons, inviting me to a meeting in their home in Irvington, New York. Nora and Motoko Sugiyama, a Japanese member assigned to a U.S. mission, would also be there.

Our church in Korea had been sponsoring sisterhood ceremonies, events creating sisterhood pairs between women of formerly alienated nations, races, and cultures. In Korea, groups of Japanese and Korean women had participated together in such moments of reconciliation.

Sitting in his spacious living room with his wife on his left, Father Moon explained to Nora, Motoko, and me that five hundred Japanese women would be coming to the U.S. in a few weeks. Noting that 1995 would mark the fiftieth anniversary of the end of World War II, he wanted to sponsor a ceremony to deepen the reconciliation between the women of former enemy nations. "Can you prepare a group of five hundred American women for a sisterhood ceremony here?" he asked.

Of course, a question like that from Father Moon was more a directive than a question, but picking up on his enthusiasm, Nora said, "Yes, Father, we will try."

Whereas the events in Korea usually involved meeting together over tea or a meal, the sisterhood meetings in the U.S. adopted the unique practice of engaging women in crossing a Bridge of Peace. This symbolized the actions of forgiveness and reconciliation between women whose nations had histories of conflict.

In January 1995, the first Bridge of Peace ceremony was held in Washington, D.C.

In the ceremony, one Japanese woman and one American

woman stood at either end of a large elevated bridge, constructed in the front of the main ballroom of one of the city's hotels. Walking toward the center, each paused and bowed to the other in a symbolic gesture of apology for the historic misdeeds of the nation she represented. Walking further forward and reaching the middle of the bridge, the two women exchanged a heartfelt hug. Holding each other's hands, they would then descend the steps together in the center of the bridge.

As each meeting took place, the song "Let There Be Peace on Earth" played in the background.

It was only a symbolic ceremony, but symbolism counts, and the participants took it seriously. The sincerity of their bows and hugs evoked something from their hearts and contributed to a spirit of reconciliation and friendship.

I was both an observer and a participant in this first ceremony. As I started across the bridge, I saw I was paired with a Japanese sister who had a kindly face and an elegant appearance. Her humble bow communicated respect and repentance, and my feeling was the same. Here I was, experiencing a genuine bond with a woman I had never met. When we hugged at the center, I felt we were indeed, on some small level, bringing two nations together.

In another pairing, an African American woman and her Japanese counterpart were moved to tears as they met in the middle. The Japanese woman wiped her tears with a handkerchief and handed it to her new sister. Later, I was told, the American sister cut the handkerchief in half, framed both halves, and sent one to Japan. "Our tears are mingled on this cloth," she wrote. "They were too precious to wash out."

Eight ceremonies were held in Washington during the first half of 1995. The experience created over four thousand Japanese-American sisterhood pairs.

World Outreach

In addition to sponsoring speaking tours by Mother Moon and holding peace-related ceremonies and conferences, the Women's Federation participated in events sponsored by other peace-related activities.

One such event, in August 1995, took place in Beijing, China, and in nearby cities. The Women's Federation participated as an NGO, sponsoring a speech by Maureen Reagan, daughter of the former president.

I arrived in Beijing from Seoul, having just attended a large Blessing ceremony. I was to meet Nora and Maureen at a hotel in the city of Haiurow, a half-hour taxi ride from Beijing.

At the hotel in Haiurow, I learned Chinese authorities had shifted my accommodation to another hotel about thirty minutes away. "But I am supposed to stay with Nora Spurgin," I said. "Miss," I heard in a sharp reply, "There are thirty thousand participants in this conference. You have been assigned elsewhere."

Not speaking Chinese and not knowing anyone who could help me connect, I wandered around Haiurow for two days looking for my team. At one point I sat at a picnic table watching a stream of women pass by.

Some did not simply pass by. Recognizing that I was an American, some women approached me to tell me sad stories of the plight of women in their countries. These were stories of rape, genital mutilation, and powerlessness. For a day and a half, I listened to such accounts.

Being lost had much deepened my understanding of the suffering endured by many members of our global sisterhood.

Toward the end of my second day, I came across a poster that said, "Celebrate the Family! Hear Maureen Reagan." That was our event. I picked up an accompanying flyer and followed the directions to the venue, happily meeting Nora, Maureen, and Women's Federation representatives from Korea, Japan, and other nations.

Maureen spoke on the connection between valuing women and valuing family. Pointing out that women around the world have been devalued, she said, "No one can value family if they don't value the role of women in them." She cited trips she had taken to Africa and India, regions where she had observed females accorded a distinctly second-class status. In Nairobi, Kenya, she had seen that young girls were the "last to be fed and the last to be cared for." Recalling a conference that she attended in India, she reported that one woman rose to explain that in her nation a woman got a bath three times in her life: "the day she is born, the day she marries, and the day she dies."

I attended other NGO sessions, one of which was particularly meaningful. It focused on helping participants identify one specific area they would like to work in, based on their interests and abilities. The presentation surfaced my interest in teaching marriage and parenting skills. Years later, Farley and I would build on our experience as marriage educators. We would help edit a book titled "Raising Children of Peace", a series of thoughtful essays by parents in our church.

Of course, when our own children went through tumultuous times, they would point to the book and tease us: "Did you raise children of peace?" We had to laugh.

Crisis

Sometimes we need to cross a bridge of peace on a deeply personal level.

"Betsy, you're late," said a fellow member on my arrival at

a Women's Federation Board meeting in New York."

"I am," I replied, "but I've got a lot on my mind." For the rest of the meeting, the business at hand floated by me like a fog. Except for a few perfunctory votes, I was disengaged.

As young adults, our eldest children, Matthew and Cara, had embraced the church tradition of arranged marriage; they were married in the Blessing ceremony I had come from when I went to Beijing.

Like any mother, I deeply wanted to see my children's lives turn out well, and my separation from my three older children made me extremely vulnerable when they were struggling. My inner hurt over having left them was never far from the surface, and I blamed myself whenever they faced difficulties.

Matthew's marriage was developing well, but Cara's was not. For various reasons, she was doubting the choice she had made, and she was in pain.

Because she was suffering, I was also.

After their marriages, Matthew continued his studies at Williams College in Massachusetts, and Cara returned to Princeton University in New Jersey. Over the next few years, Cara and her husband tried in vain to make their marriage work. Cara stove mightily and later revealed she was partly motivated by the fear that if she gave up her marriage, she would lose her parents' love.

Cara was not the only one striving. As the head of the Blessed Family Department, I was a marriage counselor. I had helped troubled couples find a path to success, and many had overcome tough challenges. Now I wanted to help Cara. I wanted to teach her the tools that had worked for others so she could find happiness.

Farley and I tried different strategies. We sent Cara and

her husband on a trip to Martha's Vineyard, went hiking with them in the Adirondacks, and offered to pay for marriage enrichment workshops.

Over time, to no apparent avail.

Why couldn't I help my daughter?

Simple. Cara and her husband were not looking for help from me.

———

After graduation, Cara surprised us all by going into the field of broadcast journalism, starting on a small scale in Boston and progressing to a job with an ABC affiliate in Fort Myers, Florida. She was a beautiful, competent young woman, and I was proud of her successes, but I was still obsessed with helping her keep her church-based marriage.

In the midst of her struggle and strain in our relationship, I visited Cara in Florida, bringing with me some empathy exercises so we could work on our relationship.

The exercises went well until we got to the topic of her marriage. I was ferocious about her staying with it, and she was equally determined that she could not. I had traveled to Florida with the intention of listening to her empathetically, but by the end of the weekend, I felt I had fallen far short; it seemed we were further apart than we had ever been. I had done more damage than good.

"Mom," she nevertheless exclaimed on Sunday night, "You're a great person!" A great person? "Cara, how can you say that?" I replied. "I've been fighting with you all weekend."

Fighting between two people who love each other can have unforeseen effects.

Resolution

Farley shared my hopes for Cara, but he was more flexible than I. Shortly after my visit to Ft. Meyers, he gave me an audio tape of a story describing the struggles of a young woman, hoping I might find some insight. I started listening to the tape one day as I was driving in my car.

The story included a comment that struck home. "I wish," said the young woman, "that I could just go to the Neiman Marcus Department store and get a mother who didn't care what other people thought." "Oh!" I thought. "I am just like that girl's mother. I have worried more about others' reactions to this difficulty than I have about my own daughter's feelings."

I had something to work on.

Rather belatedly, I decided I would turn the whole situation over to God.

My sister owns a home on Drake's Island, Maine. Most of our family had gathered there the summer following my visit to Florida, and Cara and I took a late afternoon walk on the beach. By that time, I had come to accept what was coming. "Cara," I said. "I have not been sensitive enough toward you and your pain. I will always be your mother. I want you to know I love you, and that will be true, whatever you decide."

It was a turning point.

Cara and her former husband have now both found new marriage partners.

Cara and her husband Don are the parents of a beautiful daughter.

21

Missions Abroad

In the age of jet travel and mass communications, humans can finally see themselves as "riders on the earth together," and Father and Mother Moon's global vision is timely. Those who follow them are inevitably drawn into global activism.

China was thus not the only nation I visited as a member of the Women's Federation. Over the next decade, to support connections among historically alienated groups, I traveled to Brazil, Haiti, Mexico, Russia, Israel, and the two Koreas. Some trips were brief, but visits to Mexico and South Korea involved substantial stays.

Mexico

When Father Moon was once asked if he were the messiah, he said "Yes." Then, pointing to the questioner and others present, he continued, "and so are you, and you, and you…"

In years to come, he would develop this idea further, introducing the concepts of "tribal messiah" and "national messiah." If he was to be a universal messiah, his followers were to play salvific roles on smaller scales.

In the spring of 1996, with members from around the world, Farley and I participated in a lottery held for those who had volunteered to serve as national messiahs. Our good friends, Edwin and Marie, and Hugh and Nora, were also participating.

The lottery was the culmination of a forty-day retreat held at the Cheong Pyeong Training Center in Korea, the site we had first visited with the Moons after our 1970 wedding.

In the intervening twenty-six years, the site had been developed extensively with large granite education buildings, a magnificent prayer hall, cobblestone courtyards and paved roads. It was considered to be the main retreat center for what had become the worldwide Unification Movement.

With Farley having a job, I attended the national messiah retreat, initially representing us both. Farley joined for the last ten days.

———

The forty-day program involved early rising, singing, prayer, meditation, study of the Divine Principle and, challenging all participants, a seven day fast.

Also hiking; the Cheong Pyeong retreat center was located in mountainous terrain and retreat participants had been encouraged hike frequently up a particular mountain, past trees which had received designations like "Tree of Blessing" and "Tree of Love." I have never been much into hiking and hiking that trail was not easy, particularly in the middle of my seven-day fast. Nevertheless, seeing other 777 Japanese couples who were also fasting move swiftly up the trail offered me inspiration.

One climb toward the end of the forty days proved especially significant.

Having reached the top, I stood alone reflecting on less-than-perfect aspects of my character. I then began to offer a prayer of repentance. The prayer went far deeper than I expected, and I started to weep. As I stood there sobbing, I suddenly felt a pure energy of great Love arise within me, fill me, and wash over me and simultaneously heard a voice: "I love you."

In a profound moment, I realized how much the God of infinite love loved me.

And loves all people.

———

It was after that experience that Farley arrived in Cheong Pyeong and we participated in the lottery.

The lottery's purpose was to match volunteers with nations. Sitting outside one of large education buildings under a warm afternoon sun, Farley and I waited for the lottery conductor to call our names and, not literally but in effect, pick the name of our nation out of a hat. Finally, our names were called, and our match made: Mexico!

We were more than pleased. Mexico was geographically close to the U.S., and Farley had an ancestral connection to Chile, a sister nation in the Hispanic world.

———

For Farley and me to fulfill this new role, we would again divide and conquer. He would continue his work as a lawyer, and I would assume the mission in Mexico. He would take care of the children at home, and I would witness to new spiritual children abroad. He would come to Mexico when he could.

Over the next few years, I traveled to Mexico on multiple occasions, staying sometimes for months. My work included the creation of sisterhood ceremonies between women from Mexico and from other countries, supporting a group of young Japanese sisters who had come to Mexico to engage in evangelical activities and, when either Father or Mother Moon came to Mexico to give a public talk, visiting embassies to invite ambassadors to the event.

Ultimately, we were working to make a foundation for

many couples to receive the next marriage Blessing.

To be better able to do my work in Mexico, I took Spanish language courses at a local school and tried, whenever I could, to converse in Spanish.

One summer when I could not go to Mexico, our son, Harvet, went bravely in my stead. His young, positive spirit and willingness to help were a joy for the Mexican members.

But his visit came to a problematic end.

The evangelical activities of the Japanese members had apparently not gone unnoticed by leaders of the Catholic Church, and they had apparently called upon the Mexican authorities to curb them. Early one morning, a large bus appeared outside the Mexico City church Center; members, including Harvet, were hauled off by the police to a local jail. Harvet spent two nights there before being released to return to the U.S.

Elsa, a Mexican friend whose husband was a judge, had facilitated the release of everyone.

Farley joined me in Mexico City during one of Father Moon's visits. At a members-only gathering early the morning after his speech to a large group of Mexico City residents, Father Moon suddenly looked at us and asked us to "testify about your marriage." Helped by a team who translated English to Spanish and Spanish to Japanese, we proceeded to share some of the ups and downs of our lives, the tools, beliefs and attitudes that had helped us and our gratitude for how far we had come. At the end of our talk, Father Moon smiled broadly as he gave us a thumbs-up.

He would of course be pleased. His mission was to inspire the creation of loving couples and families living in accord with the Divine Will; we were a couple who shared that goal. Despite challenges, we had made progress on the path.

Several Mexican members urged Farley and me to move to Mexico when we retired. Drawn by their warm hearts, I was attracted by the idea.

In the meantime, other work would beckon.

South Korea

As part of their peace work, Father and Mother Moon had a specific focus on the re-unification of their native country. They had both been born in North Korea, at some point had emigrated to the South and, with many other North Koreans, had left relatives behind. Further, beyond any personal concern, it was their belief that bringing North and South Korea together would have a positive global effect. A unified Korea could be a model for peace in the larger world.

In the middle of our mission in Mexico, a call came for members of the Women's Federation and other Western members to come to Korea. We were to work with Korean church members there to advance the cause of North-South reunification, and specifically to invite guests to programs introducing Reverend Moon's teachings and his vision for Korean unity.

In the moment, this task took priority over others.

For those of us who didn't speak Korean, the mission was daunting, particularly as we were to live in a Korean church center and work with Korean members.

Since I barely spoke Korean, even getting to the right church center was a challenge.

Matthew had married a Korean woman named Yunhee Jee, whose parents still lived in Korea. Yunhee's father spoke English and soon after my arrival, he and his wife took me to Koyong church, a small blue building with a red roof, built the preceding summer. Located near Incheon, northwest of Seoul, it was the area where I would live and work.

Koyong Church contained a residential space with a bedroom, bath, and kitchen. I would come to share this space with several Korean women who were participating in the campaign.

Mr. Jee introduced me to the Koyong church leader and some of the members, offered me a few sincere words of support, and said goodbye. Watching the Jee's car pull away, and able to speak only a little Korean, I felt very alone.

Before long, I decided to address the core problem. I called Mr. Jee, asking him for help in enrolling in a Korean language program. He took the necessary steps, and I was soon taking elementary Korean at Seoul's Ewha Women's University. Sharing the experience with fellow international students, and then meeting Koreans who wanted me to teach their children English, I began to feel that however long I might stay, I had connections.

At the Koyong church and beyond, I learned that if I accommodated myself to the cultural norm of bowing a little bit when I spoke, my efforts at communication went better.

With the Korean language program in place, my life took on a certain weekly rhythm: two days of language study and three days working in my assigned area; there, I passed out fliers, inviting people to attend various programs on approaches to North-South reunification. The programs were led by trained lecturers.

At the church center, I had no private life. Sharing the modest bedroom with seven other women, we slept on the floor like sardines, kept warm by Korean bedding. We hung our underwear and clothes on a shared clothesline. We got up each day at five a.m., sat in a circle on the floor, and took turns reading the Divine Principle in Korean. Though I couldn't speak Korean yet, I could read some, and I managed to stumble through when my turn came. As the weeks went by, while not knowing the meaning of the words, my pronunciation improved.

On Saturday nights, we sang to each other with the help of a karaoke machine. There was also spontaneous dancing. Encouraged one night by the wife of the pastor to sing a song in English, I settled on "You Light Up My Life." Half-way through the song, I was overwhelmed with feelings of how deeply I missed my family, especially Farley, and tears came. In that moment, I felt the depth of a love that had been growing for thirty years. How great is God!

Each Sunday, I put on my best clothes and sat for the Korean language service. About forty guests from the community attended. Since I couldn't speak, I smiled a lot.

One day, after a few weeks in Korea, I heard one of the Korean elders saying my name along with a Korean phrase, "Jo-a-hey-o." Others present nodded in agreement. I knew that "Jo-a-hey-o" meant "I like," so I could understand what they were saying: "I like Betsy." Hearing that made me very happy.

During eighteen months in Korea, I made several trips home, but most of the time I stayed on assignment. I continued studying the language, ultimately getting through levels one and two and completing a fifty-day Korean-language intensive that was intense indeed. Throughout the intensive I was helped enormously by my second daughter-in law, Harvet's wife Kori, who for the moment was living there. Having moved with her family to Korea when she was a young girl, Kori was fluent in Korean.

My investment in my area and in learning Korean paid off

when I was invited to give several brief talks at the reunification seminars. While I still needed a translator, I could give much of my talks using my partially mastered Korean. That was very satisfying.

I could have stayed in Korea indefinitely, and I had even considered proposing to Farley that we move there, as other Western members had done, but it was not to be. After the United States was attacked on September 11, 2001, the safety of international travel became uncertain, and Farley asked me to remain in the U.S. A challenging but meaningful time was behind me.

There were briefer missions. Some of the most meaningful for me were those to Israel, North Korea, and Haiti.

Israel

In May of 2004, five hundred Women's Federation members from around the world gathered in Jerusalem with the intention to help shrink the Israeli-Palestinian divide. Plans included a March for Peace and an International Bridge of Peace Ceremony.

Our March for Peace took place along a section of the Gaza strip where much conflict and suffering had taken place. We walked in silence with women from many nations attired in colorful native dress and those in the front carrying a banner identifying the marchers as "Women of Peace." As we walked on the pock-marked roadway, Palestinians of all ages stood on the roadside, watching us, smiling and clapping.

We also walked from house to house in both Israeli and Palestinian areas where we sought to engage women in conversation. We listened quietly as they shared their stories. Many women, on both sides, had suffered tremendous tragedy.

On our last day, the Bridge of Peace ceremony began with a pair of women from England and Ireland, continued with dozens of other pairs from historically alienated nations, and concluded with Israeli and Palestinian pairs. Most of the pairs earned the applause of the observers, but in a highlight of our trip, when the Palestinian and Israeli women walked the bridge, everyone stood up to clap and cheer.

Between the March for Peace in Gaza and the bridge ceremony in Jerusalem, we took a bus tour of several holy sites. In the Garden of Gethsemane, I spent a half hour in a meditative state imagining what Jesus must have felt in this place as he faced his sorrowful course. Sensing the agony underlying his prayer, "Let this cup pass from me…," I felt great gratitude for his life, his teachings, and his willingness to drink his cup of suffering for the sake of God and humanity.

North Korea

As I have mentioned, both Father and Mother Moon had separately emigrated to the South during the Korean war. Knowing firsthand the pain of families separated by political and ideological conflict, the Moons sought to establish connections with North Korea as a step toward reuniting their homeland.

In October 2007, I again traveled to Cheong Pyeong to join with seven hundred other Women's Federation members to prepare for a three-day trip to North Korea. In an unusual gesture of openness, the North Korean government had agreed to our visit.

With hearts full of anticipation, our group first stopped at the North-South border to pass through the South Korean customs process. On the other side, a set of North Korean buses took us to a nearby building where a government official gave us strict instructions: we were not to separate from the group, not to take photos except when permitted, and not to answer any questions. Any deviations from these rules by any individual would result in adverse consequences for the whole group.

Our trip through the North Korean countryside was on roads lined with imposing fences and strategically placed guards. Our destination was the Kumgang Hotel, a modern building with nearby shops and restaurants, located in the foothills of famous Kumgang Mountain.

The hotel hosted one of the highlights of our visit, a meeting in which representatives of South and North Korea made presentations on the topic of "Building North-South Unification." The content was conciliatory, leading to a moving moment at the end of the gathering when we all joined in a song of unity as each of us held a candle. Outside of this group experience, we were not allowed to speak with North Koreans, nor they with us.

Haiti

In early March of 2010, I said goodbye to Farley at the Albany County airport, heading to Haiti. A catastrophic earthquake had occurred there two months earlier. It had affected an estimated three million people, and more than one hundred thousand had lost their lives.

Perhaps I was influenced by my experience in Jamaica years earlier, but for whatever reason, I felt inspired to help. I contacted a prominent relief organization, finding out that joining its efforts required documentation that made a college application look easy.

I then heard about Evelyn, a Haitian woman who was also a member of the Women's Federation. I learned she was living in Florida, got her phone number, and called her. She had undertaken missions to Haiti before, and, yes, she was planning to return. She was leaving in three weeks.

"Evelyn, I am a nurse. How can I help?"

As it happened, Evelyn had learned from the mayor of Cap-Haitien, a town at the northern end of the island, that he needed qualified people to help those who had been traumatized by the disaster. He was looking for people to teach his countrymen to help themselves. Evelyne asked if I could present some useful seminars? Yes, I could.

As I prepared to go, things started happening. I called my friend Christine, a nurse employed at our local St. Peter's Hospital; she offered to obtain CPR teaching materials as well as bandages needed to teach first aid. I also called Cynthia, a local activist who eagerly collected medical supplies, blankets, tents, and toys. We packed and shipped these items ahead of the trip.

Before leaving, I spoke to a trauma specialist who stressed the importance of teaching breathing techniques. She also recommended healing rituals for people who had lost a loved one. After speaking with her, I decided to bring candles.

As I left for Haiti, I felt I was carrying the hearts of many who were supporting this mission.

I initially flew to Santo Domingo, in the Dominican Republic, where I met Evelyn and four others she had recruited. There were two University students from Florida and two Women's Federation members from Chicago.

An eight-hour ride took us past the Haitian border, through customs, and on to the town of Cap-Haitien where we met with Evelyn's friend, the mayor.

The mayor explained that the earthquake had been centered in Port-au-Prince, the Haitian capital. The medical facilities there had been overwhelmed, and the Port-au-Prince mayor had arranged to transport many injured individuals two hours north to Cap-Haitien. He had his work cut out for him, and he was happy that we had arrived.

Some of the medical care in the area was being supervised by two physicians, Dr. Colin and Dr. Jean. Soon after our meeting with the mayor, I met Dr. Jean and mentioned my background in psychiatric nursing. I was not a psychologist or a psychiatrist, but I was soon being treated as one. I was asked to be available to help people cope with the psychic trauma caused by the earthquake.

Dr. Jean prepared our team by telling us about some of the suffering the Haitians had experienced. I would later hear horrific stories firsthand. One woman told me her daughter, her only child, a nursing student, had fallen to her death through a large crack in the earth. Another man had lost his entire family. He could barely walk, burdened by both his injuries and his grief.

There were also victories. Two Haitians, buried for days, were finally located when rescuers fishing through rubble heard them singing hymns.

In Cap-Haitien, several of my visitors reported they could no longer sleep. I referred them to one of the doctors for sleep medication.

Because of the long line of people waiting to see me, the Haitian doctors recommended I spend only twenty minutes with each one, a very short time considering their losses.

As I met the suffering Haitians, my heart filled with love. As I listened to their stories, I would try to feel their pain. I taught them breathing exercises and emotional freedom techniques. I lit a candle and prayed for each one. In many cases, my limited efforts seemed to help.

Apart from this work, I also devoted time, as the mayor had requested, to teaching CPR to the Cap-Haitien residents. I had never worked with Evelyn's team, and I had never taught

CPR, but we successfully divided up the tasks. I taught CPR theory while other team members demonstrated the techniques. The class then practiced the techniques and asked their questions. I saw the Cap-Haitiens wanted to prepare for the future.

I was able to spend only one week in Haiti, a time far too brief, given the need. My small contribution was dwarfed by the dedication of Evelyn and of the two Haitian doctors.

22

Hawaii

The Surfer

In the late fall of 2010, finishing my work as a clinical nursing instructor at two local colleges, I decided to retire. I would miss working with students, but I wanted to see more of my children and grandchildren, some of whom lived far away. Several months later, Farley also retired. Free to travel, we eagerly planned an itinerary that took us first to Kauai, Hawaii to spend time with our son, Farley, and then on to Korea to visit Matthew and his family. I left first.

In Hawaii, young Farley O. was becoming a competent surfer, working part time in a pizza shop and doing occasional stints at farms where he could work in exchange for room and board. We had visited him once, when he was living on Hawaii's Big Island.

Also living on Kauai were our friends Mark and Sharon, who offered me temporary housing until I could find a place where my husband and I could stay when he arrived. I found Bernardo, a congenial Hawaiian who was renting a dome on his land for five hundred dollars per month. Farley O. and I could live in the dome, sharing an outdoor kitchen and shower with others living in similar small structures.

Our son's practice was to wake up early and check the ocean for surf conditions. Many days I dropped him off in the morning, coming back later to watch him surf and give him a ride home. There I cooked dinner.

Before I left upstate New York, Farley and I could see that Farley O. was having some mood changes, unlike his usual self.

Korea and Back

After Farley arrived on Kauai, we spent another two weeks there with Farley O. and then left for Korea.

By 2011, Matthew, fluent in Korean, and his wife Yunhee had been living in Korea for seven years with their then four children. Their apartment in the heart of Seoul was not huge, but even with six family members it could accommodate two more. Farley and I were happy to get there, and they were happy to welcome us. We lived with them for a sweet three months.

Soon after arriving Farley and I enrolled in a semester-long Korean language course at Ewha Women's University, a fifteen-minute bus ride from the apartment. Even though I had studied Korean there before, I could well stand to do it again. Farley and I were assigned different teachers but worked with the same textbook.

It was a time of new exploration and special closeness for us: We rode the bus, ate in the school cafeteria, went to Korean restaurants, toured Seoul, and did our homework, all of it together. In our final exams, we both scored in the nineties. With both of us then approaching seventy, we felt this was no small feat.

Toward the end of our time in Korea, we received a distress call from Hawaii's Big Island. Young Farley had experienced a decline in his mental condition following his participation in a ten-day silent Buddhist retreat. This required our presence and support. Within several days we left for Hawaii.

Luckily Farley O. had found a member of our church, Steve, at the Kona harbor, who put him in touch with the Legay family who provided housing for him until we got there. When we arrived, the Legay's took us all in for several days until we could get our own place. We will not forget their help.

We had thought our parenting work was behind us. Not true. Our son would need our continued support.

This chapter in young Farley's life turned out to be a significant chapter in our own. We had expected to return to our home in New York after visiting Hawaii and Korea, but we were now considering other options.

An unexpected encounter tipped the balance.

Decision to Move

Within the first week of our arrival on the Big Island, we learned that Father and Mother Moon would soon visit Hawaii. We were invited to join the group welcoming them to the spacious Kona home provided for them by members of our church in Japan.

As their car pulled up and the Moon couple stepped out, Mother Moon glanced at Farley and me and smiled warmly before continuing into the house. It was nice to make the connection.

Wherever Father Moon went, he would meet his followers We were invited to attend the morning meeting the day after his arrival and for several days after that.

On the second day of his visit, he began raising with my

husband the possibility of our moving to Hawaii: "Why don't you move here? You could run for governor." As other meetings went by, his suggestion that we move became more insistent. On the final day of his visit, he asked Farley directly, "Will you move to Kona?"

With young Farley in Hawaii and needing our support, we had already discussed moving. Now, Father Moon had asked us to come. Both reasons pulled us at a time in our lives when we were free to act. "OK," Farley said, "we'll move."

We flew back to our upstate New York home and prepared for a new life. In August 2011, we returned to Kona for what would be a challenging but blessed eight years.

Farley and I needed to supplement our income, and soon after arriving in Kona we enrolled in a program to qualify ourselves as substitute teachers in the Hawaiian school system. Two months later, we had both obtained our certification. I would put mine to good use as a teacher and substitute school nurse.

For Farley, different work came to him after the president of a church-related project, the Pacific Rim Education Foundation, resigned his position. Farley was asked to serve as the new president.

PREF was supervised by the Moons' daughter, Selina, and her husband, Alex Park.

In addition to substituting in the school system, I initially focused on helping Farley with PREF and trying to help young Farley achieve stability.

Intercultural Women

If in working with young Farley my spirits started to sink, I would remember things that had lifted me up in the past. This brought me to memories of activities with the Blessed Family

Department and Women's Federation. Beyond young Farley and my work, I decided I would begin my own mission with programs intended to build bridges between Hawaiian culture and the heavily Caucasian population in tourist-friendly Kona.

I started with a Hawaiian woman, Lehua, whom I had met at a church gathering. A gifted hula teacher with a loving heart, she could teach people not only the hula but also the aloha spirit that she so well embodied.

Lehua was a star attraction, and twenty guests signed up for our first meeting. Happily preparing lunch for them and learning to sway—ever so awkwardly—to beautiful Hawaiian music under a warm midday sun, I was off to a great start.

Under the banner of Women's Federation, I repeated the formula almost monthly, presenting a total of eighteen varied programs. I had plenty of help from four sisters: Michio, Myumi who were Japanese, Mary Ellen, a Caucasian, and Pohai, a Hawaiian. We were a microcosm of Hawaii's diversity, and I felt our efforts were blessed.

Our last program was a sisterhood ceremony held at Kona's oceanfront King Kamehameha Hotel, featuring a distinguished guest speaker. The eighty participants included Hawaiian hula dancers and ukulele players, Japanese sisters from Honolulu, and women originally from the U.S. mainland. Holding an interracial, intercultural event in Kona was the fulfillment of a dream.

The pain in my heart over young Farley's situation was overspread by a feeling of love for this community.

We loved the beautiful climate, beaches, flowers, trees, and ocean of Hawaii. Our work was meaningful, and we appreciated the leadership of Selina Moon and her husband Alex.

We treasured the friends we made and the aloha spirit of the islands, but all along we knew Hawaii was not our final home.

In mid-2019, ties with children and grandchildren were again calling, and it seemed that various stars were lining up for us to leave. Farley wrote to Selina and Alex to raise the idea of our moving on, and they were supportive. We had bought a house on the Big Island that we sold in record time. Young Farley agreed to move with us, and the three of us headed back to upstate New York.

23

Our Children

Each life is a story with a main character. Like their parents, our five children now have their own stories, each with unique challenges and blessings. Our lives have intersected with theirs in ways that have helped us grow in love and broaden our understanding. We are grateful to each of them.

In Asian culture an oldest son has a special role. He is to exemplify filial piety toward his parents and embody a caring heart for his younger siblings. That is Matthew.

Matthew and Yunhee have six children, three boys and three girls. They still live in Seoul, where Matthew works as an attorney in a Korean law firm, mostly representing Western companies doing business in Korea. Both he and Yunhee are avid yoga practitioners. Their children, living in Korea but going to an English-speaking school, have a clear sense of both their Korean and American heritages. Their eldest daughter chose a college in the U.S. where we are happy to see her more often. Our hearts encompass the globe every day because of Matthew's family.

I am so grateful to have a daughter! Especially Cara, who in her thoughtful, perceptive and caring way spreads love throughout our family.

In her late twenties Cara traveled extensively in South America, Europe and Asia, joined for part of her journey by Farley and me in Chile and in India by her brothers Matthew and Bow. She eventually settled in California where she became a documentary film maker and story coach. She now leads workshops, primarily on Zoom, helping others articulate their stories. Her husband Don and his brother run the successful Mountain Camp in the Sierra Nevada mountains as well as two other camps in Northern California. When not enjoying Mountain Camp during the summer, Cara and Don live in Oakland with their now five-year-old daughter.

When our son, Harvet, was about twenty, he told Farley and me he did not want to be matched by Father Moon, and that he wanted to date. This is Harv: innovative, honest, loving.

Farley and I asked him to wait a year. That year, during an unforeseen visit to Seoul, he met Kori, the daughter of another church family. Rather quickly, they decided they wanted to be married.

At that time there was no precedent for "second generation" church members to choose each other and both Kori's parents and we felt we were on very uncertain ground. Still, both sets of parents decided to test the limits and proposed their match to Father Moon. He not only approved but later announced that parents should now take responsibility for finding marriage partners for their children. That was new.

Harvet and Kori live with their three boys in a suburb of Albany, where they are successful real estate developers and have a wide circle of friends. They are great karaoke performers. As of this writing, we are blessed to live close to that family, enjoy spending time with them and watching our grandsons grow.

From early on, Bow brought us his supportive heart and creative gifts. When items-needing-complicated assembly arrived at our home, Bow was the go-to person. When a video needed musical accompaniment, Bow figured out how. When anyone needed help with anything, Bow was there, and is there now.

As a young man, he traveled throughout the U.S., leading a large team of second-generation members sponsoring rallies supporting pre-marital sexual abstinence. Bow gained the love and respect of his peers but suffered inner conflict. When the mission was over, he shared with Farley and me in a very personal moment that he was gay. That took courage; his honesty has allowed us to love him even more deeply.

Bow is everyone's favorite companion. He lives in Seattle (with his dog Arrow), works as a freelance videographer, enjoys rock climbing in the mountains of eastern Washington and has a diverse circle of close friends. He has helped his sister with some of her filmmaking and has produced videos of our family gatherings that we never tire of watching.

From early in his life our youngest child, Farley O., won all our hearts and brought us much joy. Sensitive, smart and athletic, he was recruited to play lacrosse at Tufts University in Boston. Later transferring to the Buffalo campus of the State University of New York, he took a year abroad in Brazil, having studied Portuguese on his own. There, he learned to surf.

While Farley O.'s life course has been challenging, he has displayed impressive courage and resourcefulness in dealing with it. While on the Big Island with us, he undertook a training program in massage therapy, obtained his State certification and went on to become a much-in-demand therapist. In recent times his mental health is improving. Surfing, pursued largely in Hawaii and most recently in California, remains his passion. He is a joy to watch on the waves.

Like Bow, Farley is a favorite uncle, with a gift for engaging his nieces and nephews in creative and fun activities. His course has deepened our hearts.

—⁓—

Each of our children, in his or her own way, has supported Farley and me, loving us in ways we will never forget. As a pioneering family, we suffered numerous separations, but our children tried to understand and wait with open hearts to welcome us, and especially me, back. I will always cherish their faithful love. They shared me, and Farley, with others and continue now to hold space for us in their hearts. I am in awe of each one and grateful to each one.

Now I try to stand back, allowing each one to grow on the path he or she is called to. I have struggled with the process, but as my own mother eventually let me go and trusted God, now so do I.

One thing I deeply appreciate is that our children seem to love to be with each other and with us. Like everyone, we will continue to receive blessings and face challenges. My commitment is that we will do that together. I look forward to an ever-deepening love within our family.

24

True Parents

Clasped hands

When I was a young church member in New York City, Father and Mother Moon came to visit my small apartment, the one which had become the church center. Our group made breakfast for them, doing our best to cook Korean food, and served it on a bridge table we had set up in the living room.

Our bare trappings were of no concern to the Moons. They were happy just to be with young Americans who found value in their teachings and vision. Their generous attitudes compensated for our material deficits.

After breakfast, we took them to visit the Empire State Building. Standing on the observation deck and looking out over Manhattan, Father Moon talked about the future he saw for his work in the world, including his plan for large rallies in America and in Moscow.

When the Moons left New York, driving away as we stood curbside to wave goodbye, they both turned to look at us through the car's rear window, raising their clasped hands high. Seeing this, I sensed their confidence and determination.

I felt they would bring a deep-hearted love to America and to the world; my desire to work with them grew.

Now, over fifty years later, having encountered them and having participated in their work in many situations and in multiple countries throughout the world, and having seen the hearts of innumerable men and women touched by their hearts, that initial impression has only been deepened.

Heart of God

Father Moon's family converted to Christianity when he was ten years old. This development would ultimately lead to the unfolding of an unusually sensitive, compassionate heart.

In his late eighties Father Moon wrote his autobiography. Passages in it disclose his unusual nature and report his transformative encounter with Jesus. He writes that as a young adolescent, "God [had already become] a huge presence in my life."[1] In his middle school years, reading of the suicide of a boy his same age he recalls that "With the newspaper open to that article, I wept aloud for three days and nights. The tears kept coming and I couldn't make them stop."[2] In his mountainside encounter with Jesus several years later, he reports that Jesus told him that God was "in great sorrow because of the pain of humankind...That day I saw the sorrowful face of Jesus."[3]

Through such experiences, Father Moon grasped that there is an aching dimension of God's heart and began to understand his own mission. By living a life of true love – his motto was "Live for the sake of others," by teaching the principles

---

1. Moon, Sun Myung (2010). As A Peace-Loving Global Citizen. Washington D.C. The Washington Times Foundation, p. 47

2. Ibid, p.48-49

3, Ibid, p.193

of true love ("Give, give more, and forget you have given."), by promoting the creation of God-centered marriages, and by promoting peace-related programs around the world, he would do his part to relieve God's suffering and the suffering of humankind.

He would be wholeheartedly joined in that task by his wife.

Father Moon's autobiography further recounts the story of his engagement to Hak Ja Han, younger than he by twenty-three years. He writes that after proposing marriage, including explaining to her that she would not have a normal life and that their mission would call them to a difficult path, she responded, "My heart is already set. Please do not worry."[4]

I have witnessed such depth and devotion in Mother Moon. When she and her husband came to the United States in 1971, I happened to meet her on one occasion on the second floor of Upshur House. Inviting me to a nearby room, she asked if she could sing me a song. "Of course," I said. Proceeding to lift her sweet, lilting voice, she sang in perfect English the song she had requested for the 1969 Blessing, "I Dream of Jeannie with the Light Brown Hair."

Before this, my only interaction with Mother Moon had been through a translator. Now I saw her as wanting to have a more direct relationship with me as the wife of the then American church president. As she sang this song, she was doing her part to bring East and West together. I was touched by her heart.

Mother Moon has never simply been her husband's wife. She has her own devotion to God and her own deep faith. As the founder of the Women's Federation, she has traveled the world

4. Ibid, p.193

to bring the message of true love, true family, and God's eternal ideal.

As I have mentioned, I had the privilege of accompanying her on some of her speaking tours in the U.S. As she would sit quietly praying before each speech, I witnessed first-hand her serious heart.

Included in her travels was a visit to Albany in May of 1993. Since this was Farley's hometown area, it was especially meaningful for us. Farley's father introduced Mother Moon and the step-mother of another member, my friend Alexa, also offered welcoming remarks. With the dedicated leadership of our local pastors Sebastian and Mereth, and with the support of the Barrytown community, the event drew over eight hundred guests. Later, Farley thanked Mother Moon for coming to Albany, eliciting a warm smile. Everyone likes to be appreciated!

Father Moon passed into the spiritual realm in 2012. Having shared her husband's mission for over fifty years, Mother Moon stepped into his shoes as the leader of the Unification movement.

As of this writing, she is going strong. Now known as the "Mother of Peace," she is continuing and expanding her husband's work, actively promoting family solidarity, inter-religious partnerships, and care for the earth. Most centrally she is doing everything in her power to foster the reunification of North and South Korea. Reflecting her conviction that the challenges facing the world can be solved only by placing God at the center, she has founded the "Heavenly Parent's Holy Community" as a global umbrella to embrace all people and all faiths.

Temple Bell

Father Moon died in 2012. The following poem, "Beomjeong," references a Korean temple bell noted for a sound that is said to reverberate for forty miles; it expresses one member's heart toward Father Moon:

Beomjeong
Your life is like a temple bell
that has stopped
ringing.
Yet, oddly enough
our hearts
still reverberate,
still feel your call
to prayer and service.[5]

"Prayer and service." That is the life both Father and Mother Moon led me to, on levels I could never have imagined. They have been a living temple bell, for me and for hundreds of thousands around the world.

5. Howell, Lloyd, "Remembering Father: A Poetic Tribute"

25

Fifty Years

In my final year in high school, Sister Gertrude suggested I had a vocation.

In the hours after I escaped from two men in the parking lot behind Walpole prison, I felt a call to have a large family, to an evolution from my Catholic faith and to some broad service to the family of man

And when I first heard of the Divine Principle concept of marriage, I wondered if I was led to the group to marry Farley Jones.

Somehow, through walking the unforeseen path that came to me, such intimations of my future all came to be realized in a deeply blessed way.

From the beginning I have been held in the everlasting arms of God.

How grateful I am!

In April 1992, my parents celebrated their fiftieth wedding anniversary. The highlight of the celebration was seeing them take to the dance floor surrounded by family and friends, moving together in a graceful, harmonious waltz. Knowing the trials of their life together, it was a vision that touched me. They had overcome.

The memory of seeing them dance together after fifty years is still a source of inspiration.

Farley and I reached our own fiftieth anniversary in October 2020.

I am awestruck by how much of my time with Farley has been infused with God's ever-present, mysterious grace. Even before we met, God had invested in our couple, preparing us to meet on the New Jersey shore. After our marriage He sustained us through difficulties and worked in ways that deepened our love. He shepherded two quite different people down deep valleys and over high mountains to rest now on a loving, stable, and peaceful plain.

Having the life-partner I do has been my richest blessing.

Our five children and ten grandchildren are spread throughout the world, from Albany, New York, to Seoul, Korea. We take great joy in the presence, beauty, and growth of our wonderful grandchildren, six boys and four girls.

In addition to individual visits with our children, we have maintained contact among our far-flung group by holding a family reunion each summer. Finding adequate housing for all of us, including my sister, Marilyn, has been challenging but not impossible. In recent years, we have rented spacious homes in California, from Lake Tahoe to the California Coast. The pandemic of 2020 has slowed us down, but it won't stop us! Last year we managed a week together in Cape Cod after a two-year separation.

Reunion week is filled with swims and hikes, boating and fishing, chaos and work, and connection. Long after our grandchildren have gone to bed, Farley and I retire while our adult children gather to catch up, refreshing their strong bonds.

I feel the love that indwells the generations of our family, parents to children, children to parents, sibling to sibling and grandchild to grandchild, and my heart sings.

I am filled with gratitude for those whom God has used to support me in my journey through life: my mother and father, my sister Marilyn, my husband Farley, my children and their families, Father and Mother Moon, Young Oon Kim, Marie and Edwin, Nora and Hugh, Anne and George, Therese and Ernie, Diane and George, Traudl and Shawn, the Japanese sisters, those who cared for my children: Joy, Mary and Chris, and Mark and Sharon; those who I taught and counseled, and those who have taught and counseled me; my Boston College classmates Ginny, Joan, and Kathy, and my childhood friends, Margie, Carol, and Emily.

These, and many unnamed others have been sacred gifts. I am grateful for each one.

Most of all, I thank the God who has never failed to sustain me when I could not stand, guide me in my dimness, and call me to service when I had the strength to answer.

With greater trust and faith than when I started, I will keep listening for whatever future call may come.